SECOND EDITION

STRATEGIC PLANNING FOR NEW & EMERGING BUSINESSES

A Consulting Approach

Fred L. Fry
Charles R. Stoner   Laurence G. Weinzimmer

Dearborn Trade
A Kaplan Professional Company

Editorial Director: Cynthia Zigmund
Acquisitions Editor: Robin Nominelli
Managing Editor: Jack Kiburz
Project Editor: Trey Thoelcke
Cover Design: Rattray Design
Typesetting: the dotted i

Published by Upstart Publishing Company®
a Kaplan Professional Company

Library of Congress Cataloging-in-Publication Data
Fry, Fred L.
    Strategic planning for new & emerging businesses : a consulting approach /
Fred L. Fry, Charles R. Stoner, Laurence G. Weinzimmer.
        p.   cm.
    Rev. ed. of: Strategic planning for the new and small business. c1995.
    Includes bibliographical references and index.
    ISBN 1-57410-114-5 (pbk.)
    1. Small business—Management.   2. New business enterprises—Management.
3. Small business—Planning.   4. Strategic planning.   I. Stoner, Charles R.
II. Weinzimmer, Laurence G.   III. Fry, Fred L. Strategic planning for new
& emerging businesses.   IV. Title.
HD62.7.F79   1999
658.4'012—dc21
                                                                    98-48418
                                                                        CIP

Upstart books are available at special quantity discounts to use as premiums and sales promotions, or for use in training programs. For more information, please call Upstart at 800-621-9621, ext. 4529, or write to Dearborn Financial Publishing, Inc., 155 North Wacker Drive, Chicago, IL 60606-1719.

CONTENTS

iii

LIST OF FIGURES

List of Profiles

PREFACE

Strategic Planning for New and Emerging Businesses: A Consulting Approach incorporates significant changes to the first edition, *Strategic Planning for the New and Small Business,* which was published in 1995. The first change is the updating of material and examples to better reflect businesses in the late 1990s and into the new millenium; many examples are current and highlight the needs of new and emerging businesses.

The second, and more important, change is a slight redirection of the book's major thrust. This edition, while continuing an emphasis on new and small businesses, recognizes the unique significance of emerging businesses—firms that are either in a growth mode or in the process of gearing up for growth. They represent key forces in our society. Strategic planning, while important for all businesses, is of singular importance for emerging businesses. We continue to emphasize the need for planning in new businesses, which face so many uncertainties that planning is critical. Start-up entrepreneurs are often so intent on the activities required to launch their venture that they simply don't want to spend the time looking at long-range implications. Yet understanding and utilizing a workable strategic plan can spell the difference between success and failure.

A third change in this edition is the inclusion of certain portions addressed specifically to consultants. Many readers are business managers, but a large number are consultants. Some are professional consultants who work with emerging companies to enable their growth, and some professionals are on the staff of Small Business Development Centers or similar organizations that are funded by state and federal sources to work with small businesses. Other consultants are students working on class projects specifically targeted to small businesses. Some professional consultants and students as well may be working with nonprofit organizations, which, despite lack of a profit motive, deal with many of the same pressures that businesses do and craft strategies in much the same way.

A final change in this updated edition is the addition of a third author, Laurence Weinzimmer. Dr. Weinzimmer is a colleague at Bradley University and a recognized author and consultant in the area of strategy and, more specifically, growth in organizations.

Overall, we think you'll like the second edition of *Strategic Planning for New and Emerging Businesses* even better than the original.

ACKNOWLEDGMENTS

We owe a debt of thanks to a number of people who were involved with the second edition. First, we'd like to thank David H. Bangs, Jr., Robert Brockhaus of St. Louis University, and "serial entrepreneur" Jerry Mitchell, president of the Midwest Entrepreneurs' Forum, for their words of encouragement and support.

The reviewers, Ron Christy of Wichita State University, Armand Gilinsky of Sonoma State University, Kenneth Lacho of the University of New Orleans, Charles Matthews of the University of Cincinnati, and Charlotta Nordyke of Strategic Edge Consulting, provided excellent suggestions that were implemented in the final manuscript. A number of people graciously provided feedback on their course offerings to help us prepare for the new edition. These people include the following:

R.K. Asundi, University of Puerto Rico-Mayaguez
Jane Briere, University of West Florida
Michael Broida, Miami University (Ohio)
Martha Cobb, University of West Florida
Edward Cole, St. Mary's University
Bill Cunningham, Xavier University
Frank Hall, University of Arkansas-Little Rock
Cliff Hanson, Chadron State College
William Minnis, Indiana State University
George Puia, Indiana State University
Lowell Salter, University of North Florida
Gerald Segal, Florida Gulf Coast University
Matthew Sonfield, Hofstra University
Sherrie Taylor, Texas Women's University
Charles Toftoy, George Washington University
John Wallace, Marshall University

Perhaps most important in the project was Robin Nominelli at Upstart Publishing Company, Inc. It was Robin who suggested to Upstart's management that the book be revised and updated. And it was also Robin who suggested slightly redirecting the focus toward emerging businesses. Last, we want to express our appreciation to our respective spouses—Lois, Julie, and Beth—for their support during this project.

CHAPTER 1

THE NATURE OF STRATEGIC PLANNING

This chapter sets the stage for strategic planning in new and emerging businesses. You will learn how small businesses are different from larger ones and why emerging businesses are particularly significant. You will read why planning is important for all small businesses, and you will understand why the planning process is especially critical in new and emerging businesses. You will be introduced to the planning model that forms the basis for our entire book. In particular, when you have finished reading this chapter, you should

- be aware of the need for planning;
- be able to differentiate emerging businesses from other small businesses;
- be able to identify barriers to planning;
- understand what strategic planning is and why it is important for new and emerging businesses;
- realize the benefits of planning, especially for emerging businesses; and
- understand how the strategic planning model works.

1

Perhaps no activity more fully symbolizes the American dream than owning a small business. Taking charge, exercising personal creativity and independence, risking substantial personal funds, working long hours, and planning competitive business strategies are all part of the challenge and excitement that lure one into the world of small business. But the dream of owning and operating a business can quickly turn into a nightmare of devastating frustrations if the firm's performance lags behind original projections and expectations. Although there are millions of small businesses in America today, successful growth-oriented small business ventures are the exception rather than the rule. Of the new small businesses started each year, most will struggle and many will fail within the first five years. These crushed hopes and ravaged fortunes reflect the effort of strong-willed persons who fought to build their fledgling operation into viable competitive entities—and lost.

Just as we read the horror stories of those who failed, however, we also read of the major successes of others. Names like Bill Gates, Sam Walton, J. A. Marriott, Michael Dell, and Walt Disney are examples of entrepreneurs who began businesses and grew them into mammoth organizations whose influence is felt across the country and around the globe. Thus, the failure of many is offset by the wildly successful ventures of others.

In between these two extremes are millions of businesses in America that have provided a comfortable living for their owners. Many of these businesses have remained small. At times, the decision to stay small is dictated by the competitive marketplace. There may be so many similar firms or so many with dominant market strength that opportunities for meaningful growth are limited. At other times, the decision to stay small is simply the entrepreneur's preference; the entrepreneur doesn't want to invest the time or resources to grow the business. This decision, however, doesn't minimize the need for planning. The volatile nature of current markets makes planning critical.

Some businesses have seen substantial growth over time. In fact, thousands of businesses have made millionaires of their owners. These businesses grew because the owners purposefully decided to invest the time and effort to help their business emerge from the quiet complacency of a small business into the dynamic world of a growing concern. Growth means constant change, and change demands planning. It is for those entrepreneurs who start new businesses and those owners who decide to grow their businesses that this book is written. Anyone who reads the book will certainly benefit from it, but it is the owners of new and emerging businesses that are especially the focus of this book.

THE NEED FOR PLANNING

Although small businesses encounter difficulties for numerous reasons, certain consistent themes persist. Some companies are victims of unfortunate and largely unpredictable environmental and competitive occurrences. Some simply miss their market completely. However, the vast majority of small firms fall prey to their managers' own lack of foresight. These managers don't properly analyze and evaluate their relative competitive strengths. They fail because they are out of touch with their market and don't perceive shifting consumer tastes and preferences. They fail because they lack a clear blueprint of necessary goals and support activities and therefore encounter costly duplications, overlaps, and internal inefficiencies. In short, these managers fail because they are unable or unwilling to focus on one of the prime determinants of business success—strategic planning.

Consider the following example. Bill Stern was an intelligent and industrious 28-year-old high school physics teacher. Bill felt particularly restricted and unfulfilled as a teacher and yearned for greater freedom and independence. The logical choice: start his own business. Bill was committed to working hard to make this career change a success. In exploring his entrepreneurial options, he was driven by a strong desire to do hands-on work and not be confined to the rigors and frustrations of a teaching job. Because Bill loved and appreciated motorcycles and motorcycle racing and was an accomplished motorcycle mechanic, he decided to open a motorcycle repair shop. Eighteen months later, after exhausting the family's savings and enduring a regular regimen of 60-hour work weeks, Bill recognized that the business was doomed and filed for bankruptcy.

Essentially, Bill's business decisions were spontaneous and unplanned. In the beginning, he reacted to a strong internal need for independent activity without undertaking a meaningful analysis or evaluation of his business prospects. He failed to address important questions about the actual demand for the proposed service. Bill relied on personal opinion and feeling and consequently was overly optimistic about the market potential for his business. Further, no competitive analysis was performed. Although Bill knew the names of his major competitors, he had no feel for the size of their business, the market niches they attempted to reach, or the degree of success they experienced. His repair shop was geared to the hard-core, serious motorcyclist. Unfortunately, this was the same segment of the market that his two major competitors—in terms of size and reputation—had also targeted.

Careful planning and analysis would have revealed that another large segment of the market—the weekend rider who didn't know much about motorcycles—might have been a more viable target for his business. Here, his major competition would have been dealers who generally had reputations for poor service and high prices. Recognizing this niche and exploiting it through a well-planned advertising program might have attracted numerous customers, although a careful analysis of the number of motorcycle riders in Bill's geographic area in relation to the number of competing repair shops would likely have dissuaded him from moving into this high-risk, low-potential business in the first place.

Bill's story is only one of the many unfortunate examples of good intentions and hard work undermined by a lack of solid, systematic planning. A number of research studies have demonstrated positive associations between planning and organizational performance; and inadequate planning is regularly reported as one of the key causes or predictors of small business failure.[1] Stated simply, thorough and systematic planning can significantly discriminate between successful and unsuccessful small businesses. Accordingly, the purpose of this book is to help owners and managers of new and emerging businesses, students, and consultants develop a solid, logical, strategic approach to small business planning.

The New Business

Just as Bill Stern failed to plan adequately for his new business venture, many entrepreneurs fail to do the necessary homework before starting a business. The new venture owner should at least consider the following items before launching a business.

First, potential entrepreneurs should perform a self-analysis to determine if they have "the right stuff" to run a business. Many entrepreneurs, like Bill Stern, start a business for the wrong reasons. Just because someone likes to cook doesn't mean they can run a restaurant. A person who is quite adept at building Web sites, writing code, or designing networks may make a lousy owner of a computer consulting business. Thus, potential entrepreneurs must assure themselves that they have the analytical ability, the organization skills, and the financial resources to make a business go.

Second, the new business owner must consider the nature of the competition and the environment the business will face. A market that is too small, like Bill's, will probably not succeed even if the competition is not fierce. If the business environment is riskier than usual or is dominated by larger firms, the new business will have an even tougher time succeeding. Accordingly, both the size of the market and its dynamics must be studied carefully.

Third, the availability of resources is critical for new ventures. The potential entrepreneur must carefully consider whether sufficient financial resources exist for both the start-up and later growth stages of the business. Most businesses that fail do so because of insufficient capitalization. Similarly, the new owner must consider whether an adequate, skilled workforce is available, whether the right technology is in use, and whether sufficient marketing skills exist to communicate with customers.

The Emerging Business

An emerging business is one that is growing or is poised for growth. The tasks facing owners and managers* of an emerging business who are attempting to grow the business to new levels of performance are far different from the tasks necessary to simply operate a small business at existing levels. Indeed, the culture in emerging businesses is different from that in traditional small businesses.

First, managers of emerging businesses must be proactive as they direct their thinking to the future—anticipating changes and making decisions about what is likely to occur. They must think in terms of anticipated changes in the competitive environment. They must think in terms of the financing necessary to reach new heights. They must think in terms of human and physical resources necessary to compete in the future. They must consider product and service development that will meet customer needs in the future.

Second, the climate or ambience in an emerging business is different from that of traditional small businesses. In emerging businesses, growth is the focus; it is the topic of conversation in meetings and the discussion at coffee breaks. Managers and other employees discuss competition, the industry, and the economy as a matter of course.

Consider the following example of a company that moved from being a small business to being an emerging business. Gary Erickson and Lisa Thomas owned a small business in Berkeley, California, called Kali's Sweets and Savories. It was a Greek-style bakery selling calzones and

---

*Because owners and managers in new and emerging businesses may often be the same person, we use the two terms interchangeably throughout the text.

cookies to coffee shops and groceries. On a cross-country bike ride, Erickson relied on PowerBars for nourishment. After overdosing on the PowerBars, Erickson realized that they had the capacity at Kali's to produce similar bars from all-natural ingredients. Introducing its Clif Bar, Kali's sells the cookielike bars as all-natural energy bars. Though Kali's is still small compared with the firm that makes PowerBars, it did project 1997 sales of $22 million.[2]

The difference between Kali's Sweets and Savories, the local Greek-style bakery, and Kali's Sport-Naturals Inc., the maker of Clif Bars, is one of focus. Kali's had to change its focus from a local market to a broader geographical market. It had to concentrate on the competition, on how to market the bar, and generally on how to grow. In sum, it moved from being a small business to becoming an emerging business and is on the *Inc.* 500 list of the fastest growing small businesses.

BARRIERS TO PLANNING

Even though the planning process is generally considered to be valuable, many small business owners resist planning and don't feel the need to involve themselves in the process. Although this resistance has numerous sources, a few are most prevalent. Four of the six such sources of resistance discussed in the following sections are endemic to small businesses, while the fifth is unique to new businesses and the sixth is more relevant for emerging businesses.

Barriers to Planning in Small Businesses

First, many small business owners contend that while planning may be important for large businesses, it is unnecessary for small businesses. They insist, "I don't need to plan. That's something the big boys do." This notion is an extremely dangerous form of denial. In fact, planning may be more critical for small businesses than for large ones. For example, the small business is likely to be seriously damaged by even minor market or competitive misreadings. Large firms, on the other hand, can more readily absorb the costs of such mistakes. The small business is therefore significantly more vulnerable to the consequences of poor planning.

Second, some entrepreneurs suggest that because the small business is so short-term oriented, planning for the future is only a philosophical exercise. But planning is necessary to take advantage of opportunities and defend against adverse changes and demands that exist whether the firm's planning horizon is lengthy or compressed. The small business is no better able to isolate itself from these forces than is a large firm.

Third, many small business owners feel that formalized planning confines, constrains, and limits their firm's flexibility. Indeed, flexibility, or the capacity to respond quickly and adapt to changing environmental conditions, may be the key competitive edge small businesses have over large firms. However, the assertion that planning restricts this flexibility is based on a misunderstanding of the nature and dynamics of strategic planning philosophy. Strategic plans are not unyielding parameters cast in stone, never to be adjusted, modified, or reviewed until the expiration of the operating period to which they apply. Rather, the planning process is a means of gathering information, analyzing the impact of this information on the firm, and refocusing efforts to meet new demands and conditions. As such, strategic planning offers the means to enhance rather than limit the small firm's flexibility.

A fourth frequently held view is that intuitive, unwritten plans are sufficient. A typical small firm owner may say, "I have a plan all worked out in my head, and that's good enough." Unfortunately, it usually isn't. A meaningful plan must analyze the complex interaction of numerous forces and propose a guide for how the firm will deal with these forces. Given the pressures and demands of day-to-day operations, it's unreasonable to believe that even the most insightful owner/manager can track, monitor, analyze, and develop strategies for dealing with these forces on a timely basis without relying on some formal, written, systematic process. In short, it is extremely difficult for entrepreneurs to transfer what's in their mind into sets of objective realities that guide their respective firms.

Barriers to Planning in New Businesses

Those starting new businesses are even more vulnerable than owners of existing businesses. A new venture suffers from a lack of history. Existing businesses, of course, can rely on historical data as the prelude for forecasts and planning; the previous year's data becomes the baseline for current or future years' forecasts. Unfortunately, the new business can't rely on history for help. In some cases, such as with the introduction of a totally new product or service, even industry data are not available. Without question, one of the most difficult tasks in planning for new businesses is making an accurate forecast, and, ironically, there is probably no situation in which planning is more important than in the case of a totally new venture selling a totally new product.

Barriers to Planning in Emerging Businesses

Although emerging businesses experience many of the barriers to planning noted above, they also encounter an additional barrier: lack of time. As businesses start to grow, their owners and managers become increasingly stretched for time as they are forced to spend more and more of it dealing with operational issues needed to keep up with growing demand. Thus, they don't have time for strategic planning. Frequently, they are understaffed, and their employees work long hours just to keep up with the day-to-day demands. Accordingly, planning often goes by the wayside. The planning issue for emerging businesses is so severe that one consultant attributed an estimated 95 percent of all failures in high-growth businesses to internal problems.[3]

THE BENEFITS OF STRATEGIC PLANNING

It may be intuitively clear that increases in the level and quality of planning are associated with better overall business performance, but let's examine in more detail some of the benefits of strategic planning.

The overriding benefit of strategic planning is best understood by realizing that it is a change-oriented process. New and small business owners operate in a dynamic, volatile, and ever-changing environment. Their owners must sift through, understand, and appropriately respond to the complex maze of rapid-fire changes they confront daily. Unless the owner senses the pace and direction of change, environmental shifts can overwhelm a small business operation. Strategic planning encourages a careful and systematic reading of shifts in technology, competitor position, and customer tastes. Further, the strategic planning process involves formulating actions to respond to these critical readings. As a result, change becomes a driving force of evolving strength rather than a jarring threat to stability. Consider the following example.

In an industry where similar-sized competitors have recently struggled or gone out of business at an alarming rate, Ross Marketing Services, Inc., has grown and prospered. To a large extent, that success stemmed from the company's recognition that its survival depended on strategically addressing the change within its industry.

In business for 42 years, Ross has resisted the tendency of many small advertising agencies to maintain the traditional focus on the creative side of advertising. Ross reasoned that because graphic arts were rapidly becoming computer driven, a limited creative focus would be increasingly difficult to maintain competitively. Ross paid particular attention to changing customer needs and made the strategic commitment to transform its business to be able to meet those needs more fully. As a result, Ross launched three new business units: Ross Training and Motivation (with services such as events marketing and sales promotion and training); Ross Lead Management (with services such as database management and lead generation programs); and Ross Custom Publishing (with services such as production art and technical writing).

These three new business areas, along with the core Ross Advertising, have enabled Ross to meet an array of customer demands and provide services it previously subcontracted. The focus on change continues, and Ross Marketing Services, Inc., was recently named Small Business of the Year by its local chamber of commerce. Demonstrating true strategic thinking, Ross's leaders reason that looking at new technology and blending that technology to meet evolving customer needs will continue to be the formula for success.

Beyond the broad issue of change, strategic planning offers five specific benefits. First, strategic planning helps focus on the competitive nature of the firm. Externally, the plan encourages the managers to look at the competition, the economy, the community, and other key environmental factors to determine where the firm fits. Internally, the plan forces the managers to assess the firm's strengths and weaknesses. Indeed, this analysis may reveal hidden vulnerabilities or unique strengths. As a result, necessary changes in strategy can be made. It is hoped that initial planning efforts will foster the habit of periodically reassessing the firm's competitive position. In fact, the process of carefully assessing the business and becoming aware of its potential and capacity may be even more significant than the plan that is eventually derived from this analysis.

An example illustrates this point. A local businesswoman had been regularly counseled by a business consultant to develop a plan for her growing operation. She was, of course, quite busy and never got around to it. One day the woman rather excitedly reported, "Guess what, I've started on my plan, even though I haven't finished. But one night while working on it, I suddenly discovered a problem in the business that I corrected the very next day." Because this businesswoman had begun to prepare a plan objectively, she uncovered a correctable weakness she had not seen before.

A second benefit is that a strategic plan sets a formal direction for the business. It helps determine where the business is going. In addition, and perhaps as important, it helps determine where the firm is *not* going. Thus, a plan helps owners focus on specific objectives and stay there. This planning orientation allows small business managers to work proactively, looking to the future and anticipating and planning for change. Managers of proactive firms anticipate opportunities and position themselves to benefit from them. Similarly, these managers recognize impending threats and take decisive action to deal with them before disaster strikes. Crisis management is replaced by a more fluid, logical, and systematic approach. The firm's management understands and treats change as a competitive weapon rather than as an uncontrollable nuisance to be ignored as long as economically and competitively possible.

The following example highlights the importance of competitive awareness and focus. An extremely enterprising young man possessed classic entrepreneurial flair. He was involved in three different business ventures and personally headed a firm that operated in such diverse areas as insurance, real estate, and managerial consulting. Not surprisingly, he was experiencing problems in nearly all phases of his businesses. One might logically assume that the underlying cause of his difficulties was his attempt to do too much—spreading himself too thin. Although he *was* spreading himself thin, his difficulties stemmed from a total disregard for formal planning. He failed to provide a clear view and direction for each business. No attempt was made to prescribe what needed to be accomplished, when, and by whom. He simply reacted and allocated his time and his firm's resources toward the most pressing problem of the day. Consequently, most efforts were temporary fixes that added little to the development of his firm. In addition, he regularly missed important and potentially rewarding bids and contracts because his focus was on putting out yesterday's fires rather than looking for tomorrow's opportunities. Strategic planning helped the man understand his total business better and develop some concrete moves to enhance his competitive position. Because what needed to be done was now clear, meaningful delegation was possible. The young businessman was free to concentrate on making contacts, meeting potential customers, and engaging in the necessary public relations work he was uniquely qualified to perform. Important opportunities were realized and acted on, and internal operations ran more smoothly.

The above example suggests a third benefit of strategic planning. As the firm's direction became clearer, employees were allowed to make decisions. They were allowed to use their skills more fully. They became surer of themselves and more comfortable in their roles, and their jobs were enriched. Most workers have a strong desire to know what's going on and how their efforts contribute to the overall business objectives. Without a clear notion of these objectives, employees are often frustrated and dissatisfied. Planning helps employees become part of the organizational team. As employees know more of what the owner has in mind, they become more motivated, more willing to suggest ideas, and more willing to exert the extra effort needed to give the business an edge over the competition. Because a small firm in particular is competitively vulnerable, its employee efforts and suggestions often make the difference between success and failure. Indeed, as business leaders clearly communicate direction, philosophy, and objectives to their workers, the returns are likely to be dramatic.

Fourth, a business plan is useful to the board of directors or the advisory board. These members are not involved with the day-to-day operations of the firm even though their job is to offer guidance and advice. The plan gives them a basis for analyzing, evaluating, and making suggestions for the firm's overall operations.

Finally, the existence of a formal, overall strategic plan makes the creation of special-purpose plans, such as those for financing, much easier. In fact, the strategic plan contains most of the information used in developing specialized plans. Although a manager may feel that planning is difficult and time-consuming, the impact of the planning process is overwhelmingly positive.

THE STRATEGIC PLANNING PROCESS

Dwight D. Eisenhower once said, "Plans are nothing; planning is everything." While we would question whether the strategic plan itself is nothing, it certainly is true that planning is everything. Although it is important for all businesses to have a written plan, the strategic planning process—the focus of this section and the basis for the rest of the book—is critically important for new and emerging businesses.

Defining Strategic Planning

Strategic planning is a powerful management tool designed to help new and emerging businesses adapt to anticipated environmental changes. More specifically, the strategic planning process provides an overview and analysis of a business and its relevant environment. It describes the firm's current condition and recognizes the key external factors affecting its success. The process then prescribes an outline, or action plan, of how the business will proceed to capitalize on its strengths and minimize its weaknesses and threats.

Although business managers are occasionally asked to write business plans in order to secure financing, these should not be confused with strategic planning or strategic plans. Investment-oriented business plans are single-purpose documents. As such, they tend to be very specific, reasonably brief, and somewhat optimistic overviews of the business, its product line, its management, and the proposed use of funds. By contrast, strategic plans require more depth and breadth of coverage. Their focus is the future. They consider internal strengths and weaknesses, for both may affect the strategy selected. They are regularly used and frequently revised to reflect new trends and developments. The strategic plan is both an analytical tool and a working document that guides management action over a specified period of time.

Determining the Planning Horizon

The noted economist John Maynard Keynes once said, "In the long run, we are all dead." We need to be more specific than that in determining the short-term, medium-term, and long-term goals for a firm! In general (but not always), long-term planning refers to anything beyond the next five years. A three-year period is often the target for medium-term plans. Short-term plans are generally for one year or less. Accountants, on the other hand, often refer to anything over one year as long range.

Actually, the determination of long-range versus short-range goals is a function of the industry and the type of product or service. A utility company necessarily looks 15 to 20 years ahead because of how long it takes to build a power plant; a small janitorial service may have no reason to look beyond a year; and a small manufacturer looks somewhere in between.

The above examples introduce a key factor in planning—the firm's planning horizon. The planning horizon is the time required to implement a major strategic change. Beyond that time period, a manager need only do some casual monitoring because the business can react to any change that might develop.

Suppose, for example, I own a restaurant. I could spend a considerable part of my time studying new housing developments and specific projected growth areas of the city. On the other hand, the total time required to build a new restaurant is probably between six months and one year. Because migration is a relatively slow process, I'll have ample time to study site locations once I determine that I do, in fact, need to expand.

Remember that strategic reaction time is the concern here. The environment must always be monitored to determine developing trends. But serious study need only be done when either a strategic change is desired or when significant changes in the environment dictate study. Attempts to react to each minute change will lead to overreaction and/or unnecessary concern with the long run when it cannot be adequately assessed, as shown in the following example.

An Italian restaurant had an excellent reputation for good, moderately priced food, but its location and size eliminated a major portion of the city's population as potential customers. The owner adroitly decided to add a new location in a growing section of the city, close to a major shopping mall. The move was handled well, and profits flourished because there were few similar restaurants in the area. Less than three years later, the competitive environment had changed drastically. Two national restaurant chains featuring Italian cuisine opened in the same area of the city. Two other restaurants opened at sites within two blocks of the restaurant. At first glance, this would appear to be a classic case of bad planning. Shouldn't the owner have been able to predict three to five years in advance? The answer is no. Even though the restaurant is now in a highly competitive market, no way could the increased competition have been projected. The changes were outside the manager's strategic reaction time. The planning horizon was not that distant and should not have been expected to be. The move was a wise move at the time.

If managers extend the horizon too far, they may lock themselves into a strategy that later becomes inappropriate. If the horizon is too short, opportunities may be missed. Underestimating the planning horizon is the more frequent error. Most firms tend to concentrate on the short term, and we often encourage managers to look farther out into the future. Many managers are so busy fighting fires that they don't take time to consider needed changes within their planning horizon. Managers must consider how long it will take to react to a change in the environment and plan accordingly.

Planning and forecasting are especially difficult for both new and emerging businesses. In both cases, the firm is being taken into uncharted territory. However, it is critically important for managers to attempt to assess the dynamics of the environment being faced. Only when an accurate analysis of the competitive environment is made can the owner or manager of a new or emerging firm make decisions that are logical and defendable.

THE STRATEGIC PLANNING MODEL

Figure 1.1 highlights a strategic planning process for new and emerging businesses. The process is comprised of three phases. The *premise phase* occurs as the manager looks toward the future and formulates a vision for the business. This phase also includes the development of a mission that provides a broad direction and philosophy for the business.

During the *analysis phase,* managers go through a number of steps to assess the business's environment and determine its strengths and weaknesses. They must develop a list of the key threats and opportunities in the firm's relevant external environment by studying present environmental forces, by projecting trends, and by anticipating changes. Managers must not only identify and track changes in key environmental factors, they must carefully assess the impact these forces and changes will have on the firm and its operations. Environmental analysis is therefore future oriented, seeking to recognize the problems and potential created for the firm by changes in its environment.

Whereas environmental analysis concentrates on forces external to the organization, internal firm analysis evaluates the firm's internal strengths and weaknesses. An astute manager will study a number of important issues as part of determining the strengths and weaknesses of the business. These will include assessing the financial status of the firm, analyzing human resource needs, studying marketing capabilities, and determining the ability of the company to produce a quality product or service.

FIGURE 1.1   <u>STRATEGIC PLANNING MODEL</u>

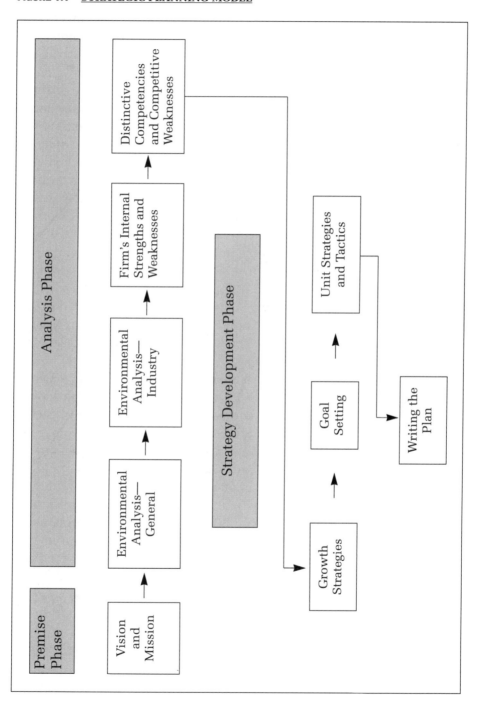

Environmental and internal analyses enable the firm to portray carefully and objectively both its special competencies and its relative competitive weaknesses. A distinctive competence is any area in which the firm possesses a meaningful edge over its competitors. Similarly, competitive weaknesses represent areas in which the competitors' relative strengths are significant or overwhelming. Armed with this information, the manager can realize and capitalize on evolving competitive opportunities (distinctive competencies) and develop protective measures to minimize the harmful impact of materializing threats and obstacles (competitive weaknesses).

After environmental and firm data have been analyzed and evaluated and the firm's distinctive competencies and competitive weaknesses delineated, the manager is ready to embark on the *strategy development phase* of strategic planning. Here, the manager uses the results of the environmental and firm analyses, contemplates the implications, and structures a working plan to guide the firm's activities.

The first step in the strategy development phase is to determine the overall growth strategy for the business. How much growth is desired? How will the firm compete? What will be the primary strategic thrust in the near future? This first step is a logical, functional, and integral process that can guide the firm along the path of success.

Once the firm's overall growth strategy is established, the manager of the emerging business will then focus on specific goals. Setting achievable and measurable goals for the company as a whole and for operating units or divisions is an important process.

Unit strategies breathe life into goals. Essentially, a goal statement declares what a business wants to do or wants to be, while unit strategies declare how the business is going to do it. Decisions to segment the market, change pricing, alter sales methods, acquire additional funds, and change production methods are examples of unit strategies undertaken to move the firm toward the realization of its goals.

The best strategies in the world are of limited value if they are not written down. Our final chapter presents and discusses a format for the written plan. Appendix A contains an example of a completed strategic plan based on a real business that can be used as a guideline for developing a plan for any business.

Figure 1.2 is a sneak preview of the strategic plan format. As you move through the book, you may want to refer back to Figure 1.2 to see how the actions discussed fit into the final strategic planning document.

FIGURE 1.2   <u>STRATEGIC PLAN FORMAT</u>

I. Vision statement

II. Mission statement
   A. Product line or services provided
   B. Philosophy of the business

III. The business and its environment
   A. General environment characteristics
   B. Industry environment and competition
   C. Location description

IV. Distinctive competencies

V. Growth strategies and goals
   A. Company-level strategies
   B. Company goals
      1. Horizon goals
      2. Near-Term goals

VI. Unit-level goals and strategies
   A. Marketing
      1. Target market
      2. Product mix strategy
      3. Pricing strategy
      4. Promotion and selling strategy
      5. Distribution strategy
   B. Operations
      1. Facilities
      2. Make-or-buy decisions
      3. Lease/purchase of equipment
      4. Vendor selection
   C. Human resources
      1. Employment strategy
      2. Promote from within versus hiring outside managers
      3. Wage/salary/benefit strategy
   D. Financial
      1. Debt/equity strategy
      2. Capital sourcing strategy
      3. Growth/stability strategy
      4. Financial projections

VII. Target Goals and Target Action Plan

THE CONSULTANT'S VIEWPOINT

Each chapter concludes with ideas, guides, and a few caveats for those who are consulting with business owners in addition to the Focus in Chapter 2 on managing the consulting process. Even though some readers may be students in a small business consulting class, some may be consultants, and some may be owners or managers of emerging businesses, we hope that "The Consultant's Viewpoint" section in each chapter provides food for thought to all readers.

Enabling the Planning Process

Two partners of an emerging business once approached one of us with an offer to pay (presumably big bucks) for writing a business plan. Consultants should never take that on as an assignment, and business owners should never ask. It *is* wise, however, to ask consultants to *facilitate* the planning process.

Note the difference between consultants writing a plan and facilitating the planning process. Consultants should enable planning, but they should resist writing a plan for a business owner for one key reason. For planning to be effective, the business owner must be actively involved. It is useful to draw upon a consultant's expertise, but the plan has to have the imprint of the owner. The owner is the one with intimate knowledge of the company's strengths and weaknesses and most likely knows the industry better than the consultant. The consultant's role is to draw out all this information in an interactive manner and assume an objective role during deliberations.

Plans versus Planning

The Eisenhower quote a few pages earlier is the key to the issue of plans versus planning. If the planning process does not result in a document that can be referred to and used for future reference, the process is of minimal value. However, if the focus is on the document instead of the process, the task will be shortsighted and incomplete. It is the planning process that uncovers new information. The process ensures that an objective analysis of the firm is done. The planning process results in alternative strategies for the business that can then be considered before implementation. Only once the planning process has been done carefully can the written plan become a guide for action.

Communicating the Plan

If the planning process has been done well, key managers in the emerging business should be aware of the strategies being developed. Indeed, they will have been involved in that process. But others in the company also need to know what the firm's strategy is. Employees in a production facility can better understand their role in the company if they can understand where the company is headed. The sales force can sell the firm's products better if they know how those products are positioned compared with competitors' products. Even the morale of staff workers should be better if employees fully comprehend the mission and vision set by the owners, especially true in the emerging business because all members will likely be under stress. A strategic plan is primarily used to guide the direction of the firm. But don't underestimate the power of a well-written, well-communicated strategic plan as a motivating tool.

DISCUSSION QUESTIONS

1. Why is strategic planning perhaps even more important for a small business than it is for a large business? Why is it critical for emerging businesses?
2. If planning has so many benefits, why don't small business owners do it?
3. Choose a firm with which you are familiar. What specific benefits could arise from doing formal planning in that particular firm?
4. Estimate the appropriate planning horizon for the following:
   a. a software development company
   b. a bowling alley
   c. an auto repair shop
   d. a manufacturer of circuit boards for high-tech diagnostic equipment

5. Explain how the major parts of the planning model could be used in the following:
    a. national planning for a country
    b. individual career planning

NOTES

1. For example, see LuAnn R. Gaskill, Howard E. Van Auken, and Hye-Shin Kim, H. "Impact of Operational Planning on Small Business Retail Performance," *Journal of Small Business Strategy,* 5(1), 1994: 21–36; LuAnn R. Gaskill, Howard E. Van Auken, and Ronald A. Manning, "A Factor Analytic Study of the Perceived Causes of Small Business Failure," *Journal of Small Business Management,* 31(4), 1993: 18–31; and Charles R. Schwenk, and Charles B. Shrader, "Effect of Formal Strategic Planning on Financial Performance in Small Firms: A Meta-Analysis," *Entrepreneurship: Theory and Practice,* 17(3), 1993: 53–64.

2. Joseph Rosenbloom, "Follow the Leader," *Inc.,* October 21, 1997, p. 83.

3. Stephanie Gruner, "Death By Unnatural Causes," *Inc.,* October 21, 1997, p. 62.

Managing the Consulting Process

In examining strategic planning from a consulting perspective, key planning themes are not only specified and explained, but careful attention is given to how business consultants can use strategic planning tools as they interact with client businesses. Subsequent chapters provide guidance on how topics can be approached to build client rapport and generate meaningful and usable strategic plans. This chapter introduces some general guidelines for consultants that are important when they're working with new and emerging businesses. These guidelines will help to create good consultant-client relationships and to manage the overall consulting process. After reading this chapter, you should be able to

- understand the unique nature of consulting with new and emerging businesses;
- recognize the various types of consulting that are frequently encountered;
- understand the importance of building rapport and be aware of approaches that can help this process;

- recognize how the problem definition stage of the consulting process can be handled;
- understand some of the details and complexities involved in gathering and analyzing data; and
- have in mind a format for making recommendations to clients.

Consulting with new and emerging businesses can be an exciting and challenging experience, allowing consultants to put their knowledge of strategic planning to use in concrete situations. No longer merely an academic undertaking, strategic planning becomes a mechanism for helping real people deal with real business issues. The twists and complexities encountered in this process are always somewhat novel. The frustrations are numerous. But the rewards derived from helping owners of new and emerging businesses grasp and deal with their competitive situations are significant and far-reaching.

As we noted in Chapter 1, some readers are professionals, some want to start a consulting business, and some—the majority, we suspect—are students in business classes at colleges and universities. Among the students, some are in a typical small business management course or an entrepreneurship course, whereas others are in consulting classes where much of the focus is on the consulting experience. A significant percentage of these consulting students are in a program known as the Small Business Institute™ (SBI), which was funded by the U.S. Small Business Administration for more than 20 years. Although that funding has since been eliminated, the program continues to exist in many colleges and universities with funding provided by the college or other sources. Some institutions now refer to the program simply as a business consulting class, a senior project class, or a small business analysis class. Indeed, clients for many projects are not businesses at all but rather are nonprofit organizations. Technically, these are not businesses because they lack the profit motive, but the consulting process is much the same.

Because the results of consulting can mean the difference between a business's continued growth and its stagnation, the consulting process can never be underestimated. Indeed, a consulting project can sometimes mean the difference between the continuation of the business and its termination. Consider the following examples. A student consulting team once worked with a business whose owners requested a complete internal and competitive analysis along with precise recommendations of what should be done to reverse a downward spiral in revenues. The students realized that the business owners, a middle-aged husband and wife, were nice people literally at their wit's end. One student noted, quite appropriately, "These clients are depending on us. They intend to do whatever we tell them. It's kind of scary to think we are going to play a key role in the fortunes of these people and their livelihood." When another team presented its final report to the client, the client informed the team that it had reinvigorated his desire to run his business. He had never told them before that he was really planning to sell the business. Now, however, because of their interest and suggestions, he was enthusiastic about continuing and growing his business.

Certainly, all consulting interventions do not hold the same dramatic prospects these students faced. Yet working with owners and managers of new and emerging businesses poses unique demands and can be intimidating. At the same time, business owners and managers must realize that consultants are only advisers. They do not dictate what the owner must do, and owners are under no legal pressure to accept what consultants recommend. Because each party to the consulting process should have realistic expectations about both the process and its possible results, the nature of consulting and a recommended four-phase consulting process are examined in the following sections.

THE NATURE OF CONSULTING

Clients typically seek consulting assistance for one of two reasons. The first is that the company is experiencing some type of problem. The manager may or may not even be aware of what the real problem is but knows that something is wrong. The owner asks a consultant to study the business objectively, identify problems and areas of concern, determine causes of the problems, and recommend solutions.

The second reason for using a consultant may be more relevant for new and emerging businesses. In these cases, the business is growing but clients need assistance in enabling the growth. Clients recognize that growth, left unchecked and unplanned, can be disastrous in a dynamic, competitive environment. Consider the following example.

A dentist had an excellent practice involving two offices, another dentist, and a number of hygienists. After several years, the dentist decided it was time to grow by taking advantage of a trend in his profession of buying existing practices as current owners retired. In addition, the dentist felt that an additional service—dental implants—could be provided to baby boomers and senior citizens. With these two goals in mind—expanding the number of offices and expanding the types of ser-vices offered—the dentist called a consultant, who provided help in two areas. First, the consultant conducted focus group research to determine the willingness of senior citizens to accept the concept of dental im-plants. Second, the consultant spent considerable time with the dentist's growing company to develop an organizational structure and common organizational culture for the entire company.

Consultants can provide an objective analysis of opportunities. And not only can they provide candid interpretations of internal operations, but they also can help managers of new and growing companies control business growth so a stable financial condition is maintained as the com-panies grow.

Types of Consultants

The first type of consultant is the large consulting firm such as An-dersen Consulting, Hewitt Associates, or PricewaterhouseCoopers. Large firms often have specialties in addition to doing general consulting. An-dersen, for example, specializes in information systems, while Hewitt specializes in employee benefits.

The second category is the small consulting firm, which may consist of only one or two individuals and a support staff. These firms, too, may be either specialists or generalists. Some firms, for example, specialize in business valuation. Some may offer accounting services primarily, and still others may be small market research firms.

A third type is the part-time consultant who has another job but does consulting on the side. Many business professors do consulting in their areas of specialty and are even encouraged to do so by their universities. Some part-time consultants work for large companies and do consulting after hours. For example, a person who works in the information systems area of a hospital may moonlight as an information systems consultant.

The fourth kind of consultant is the not-for-profit organization. Non-profit consulting organizations, such as those underwritten by the Small Business Administration (SBA), provide free or low-cost consulting ser-vices by staff, volunteers, or students. The Service Corps of Retired Execu-tives (SCORE) is comprised of retired volunteers who previously worked in business and whose minor expenses are covered by the SBA. Another SBA-funded operation is the previously noted Small Business Develop-ment Center, which typically receives both state and federal funding in order to provide staff consultants to area businesses. Universities often have some form of consulting course or project for their students, who gain extensive hands-on consulting experience while providing supervised consulting to hundreds of small companies each year. In addition to SBA-sponsored consulting, many universities have some type of center for business research that provides fee-based consulting. Businesses request and may receive specific consulting help from a research center; consulting fees and contract terms are then determined. At times businesses indicate their consulting needs and encourage the submission of bids so that the university research center is only one of many consulting possibilities for businesses. Other not-for-profit and trade associations also provide consulting either free or for a modest fee.

Types of Consulting Projects

Just as there are many different kinds of consultants, there are many different types of consulting. In a one-time presentation to a client or client group regarding some business topic, the consultant makes a speech to a client group or holds a seminar on some topic. Presentations often pay modestly, but such engagements may lead to more one-on-one consulting from members of the audience. A second type of consulting is technical consulting in which the consultant provides expert information to clients. This, too, may lead to additional engagements. Third, consultants often will be called in to do extensive market research for clients, in which case a significant amount of hours may be billed either on a per-hour or flat fee basis. Finally, consultants may facilitate the planning processes of a client company by meeting on an ongoing basis with the client and key members of the client's organization. The consultant helps the organization determine a vision, set strategies, or solve significant problems.

THE PHASES OF THE CONSULTING PROCESS

The four phases of consulting, discussed below in detail, are the rapport-building phase, the problem identification phase, the data-gathering phase, and the recommendations phase.

Building Rapport

No matter how talented consultants may be, those talents are only recognized and appreciated by clients when a base level of rapport and trust is established. Some clients are, by nature, open and accepting people—others more guarded and uncertain. All clients, however, must have confidence in their consultants if they are to work with them to produce valued changes in the business. When a manager engages a consultant, that manager is entrusting certain business revelations and outcomes. For most small business owners, who have a tendency to value independence and self-sufficiency, this act of trust is not taken lightly nor entered into without serious deliberation. The consultant must act to build rapport, ensure confidence, and establish a working foundation of trust.

Confidentiality. Business clients need assurance of confidentiality. The consultant must explain to the client that all information received about the business will be treated with strict and absolute confidence. If there are exceptions to this statement, those exceptions need to be delineated and explained at the time of engagement. For example, a student consulting team routinely has to share information with the faculty member directing its project. Consultants must present their claims of confidentiality in a serious and convincing manner if they are to win the acceptance of their clients. More important, it is the professional and moral responsibility of consultants to abide by the terms of the confidence they have guaranteed.

Competence. The underpinning of confidence and trust rests on competence. If clients feel that consultants are skilled and knowledgeable, they are more likely to reveal and share information and ideas. Consultants must provide information to clients that communicates competence. Student teams sometimes have difficulty here, but they may find that providing résumés showing classes completed and jobs held may add to their credibility. Professional consultants may also encounter a fear of their incompetence among clients. Consultants should communicate their areas of expertise to clients in initial meetings so that clients will feel comfortable with the consultants' level of competence.

Deadlines and commitments. Confidence and trust are built incrementally through seemingly small actions. A key initial factor here is the way deadlines and commitments are honored. If a consultant tells a client that a summary of the initial meeting will be prepared by Tuesday, the summary must be delivered by Tuesday. If a consulting team agrees that the entire team will meet with the client at 6:00 PM Friday, the entire team should be there. Such small commitments are the primary way that a client can judge whether the consultant will treat more sensitive and significant revelations with appropriate scrutiny and diligence.

It is also important that a consultant not make commitments he or she can't keep. A business owner, on the other hand, should recognize that a consultant is busy and the owner's business is only one of the consultant's many responsibilities. Both client and consultant must be clear and up front about expectations and schedules.

Establishing confidence between client and consultant is the real key in the rapport-building phase. Keep in mind, however, that the level of confidence and trust between the two must be ongoing. Every contact and every interaction between client and consultant should continue to instill and build confidence.

Defining the Problem

Early in the consulting relationship, business managers should be encouraged to define their problems or needs as carefully as possible for two reasons. First, defining their problems forces owners to think through the factors and issues they are confronting, often providing valuable input and information the consultant can use. Second, it often helps clients move beyond symptoms, pushing beneath the surface to reveal underlying causes of organizational problems. This presumes, of course, that clients are aware of their needs, which sometimes is not the case. In fact, clients' awareness of their needs, when it exists, is a key factor in problem definition.

Problem awareness. Frequently, small business clients are aware of their needs but simply don't have the expertise to address them. Owners of new and emerging businesses have an additional problem: They may be aware of their needs but may not have the time for the necessary analysis and implementation. For example, a client may be aware that current advertising efforts are woefully inadequate and yet be so embroiled in day-to-day operations that there is simply no time to analyze and develop a well-orchestrated advertising plan. Or perhaps, even more typical, a client may have adequate technical expertise in the design and manufacture of a product but virtually no understanding of, nor interest in, the dynamics of the marketing function. In such situations, the client understands the strategic necessity of getting help and thus decides to entrust a certain area of business to a consultant's expertise.

It is not unusual, however, as the consultant engages in the details of strategic analysis, to uncover concerns and needs that the client didn't know existed. Then the consultant's first task may be to educate the client. Generally, this means that a client must not only be told that an unrecognized need exists but must also be convinced that the need is real. The best way to convince clients is to show them clear, documented evidence. Business owners respond to the bottom line, and if they can be shown the bottom-line implications of dealing with a problem, the likelihood that they will go along with a solution is greatly enhanced. For example, showing a client that the firm's financial ratios vary dramatically from industry averages may encourage the owner to pay attention to what is causing the variance.

Care must be exercised at this stage. Some clients feel threatened when consultants uncover new concerns and problems. Often, clients' pride and ego are bruised, so consultants, therefore, must be firm but supportive. Consultants must convey a positive image that encourages clients to accept the issues and become part of the plan to remedy the problems.

Statement of work.   At a point early in any consulting intervention, a clear statement of work should be developed by the consultant and presented to the client. While responsibility for drafting the statement of work rests with the consultant, the development of the statement cannot be a unilateral effort. The client must contribute to the development of the statement, and points of disagreement must be discussed and negotiated. The consultant must understand the client's business situation and relevant issues to such an extent that the statement responds meaningfully to the needs of the business.

In all likelihood, some problems will not be addressed. Rather, consultants may select particular areas in which immediate action is necessary. Or they may select areas that mesh best with their own background and experience. Or they may select areas in which it is clear that owners don't have the time or expertise.

The statement of work becomes an agreement between the parties that outlines the nature and scope of the consulting that will be performed. This statement establishes and formalizes each party's expectations of the other and should clearly indicate the type of work to be done. However, it will not and cannot, at this early juncture, prescribe many of the specifics and details that will no doubt occur during the consulting process. The statement should be rather broad, while still defining the topic of coverage. For example, if a client is seriously questioning the effectiveness of current advertising approaches, the statement may focus broadly around the issue of advertising. The consultant may indicate that "an evaluation of the current advertising strategy will be performed and appropriate changes will be recommended." Although such a statement provides the consultant with considerable flexibility in terms of approaches and execution, the client clearly knows what outcomes to expect.

Gathering and Analyzing Data

The common cliché in woodworking to "measure twice, cut once" is equally good advice for consultants. Consultants who do a thorough job of gathering data and analyzing that data (measuring twice) will have a more successful relationship because their solutions (the cut) will be better. Although detailed techniques of data gathering are presented in Chapter 4, some general themes are introduced here.

Preparation.   Consultants have no alternative to hard work and diligence. They must be thoroughly prepared when meeting with clients. For most business owners and key managers, the most precious and limited resource is time. Nothing frustrates owners more or is more destructive to the client-consultant relationship than the client's perception that his or her time is being wasted.

Consultants must review documents and know as much as possible about clients before an initial meeting. They should understand what they already know and what they must learn. And they must coordinate their questions so that client's time is used most effectively. Consultants often study a client's industry in some depth (faculty members often require this of student teams) so that during an initial meeting they are knowledgeable about the client's industry and the firm's place in it.

Listening.   When consultants meet with clients, it is critical to let the clients talk. Often, consultants—especially student teams—think they have to impress clients with their knowledge and background. While some of that is necessary to build client confidence, many consultants are reluctant to step back and let clients express their views and impressions. Consultants must listen to what clients say, and they should take notes to have a record of points to ponder and evaluate after they leave.

Consultants should ask questions about areas of confusion or areas where more focus needs to be exerted to help clarify both the problem and possible solutions. For example, if a client says she is having difficulty securing funds, probe for her impressions of why she is experiencing difficulty.

Communication. One of the most common client complaints is that consultants don't let them know what is being done and what progress is being made. It's critical for consultants to keep their clients well informed. Often, consultants are working hard analyzing data and searching for information and see no reason to contact their clients. Clients, unaware of what's being done, perceive lack of contact as lack of interest. Consultants should have regular informational updates with clients. The schedule and frequency of updates is really a function of both consultants' and clients' needs. The contact does not always have to be in person, but it must occur. Because credibility and trust are built over time, contacts become building blocks of the consultant-client relationship.

Search for practical answers. Seeking practical solutions is one of the greatest challenges consultants face. Frequently, consultants, assuming that resources are unlimited, search for ideal and optimal ways to address client concerns and needs. Unfortunately, new and emerging businesses rarely operate in an ideal world, which in no way suggests that the consulting analysis should proceed without careful scrutiny and rigor. However, a consultant must always be aware of the realities the client faces. Such realities as depleted finances, tight cash flows, and short-run commitments to existing technology may limit possible solutions. Inadequate cash and frequently changing technology are two of the most significant problems facing growing businesses. Solutions that ignore these issues will be shortsighted.

The preferred solution may do little to advance a business in its strategic efforts. Shenson and Nicholas note that successful consultants suboptimize—that is, realize that an optimal solution may be too costly to be reasonable and practical.[1] Consultants must propose the best solutions possible given the constraints of time, money, and resources.

Making Recommendations

A successful consulting engagement culminates in recommendations being shared and understood. This does not presume that owners and consultants will always agree. Nor does it assume that clients will act on and implement all recommendations. Rather, clients must understand the complexity of a consultant's recommendations and the reasoning behind them.

Final written report.　After conducting all analyses and determining what recommendations to make, a consultant must formalize his or her conclusions and rationale in a written document to be presented to the client. Prescribing the exact form and content of this document is difficult and is largely a function of the nature and scope of the project. In the case of student consulting projects, the supervising faculty member may prescribe the final report format. Yet certain themes should be considered and included in the written report as outlined in Figure 2.1.

The report must be written to the client and for the client. Thus, the tone of the report should take the client's background and level of comprehension into consideration. If the client is likely to be unfamiliar with specific jargon and terminology, a consultant should avoid those phrases even though they may be accurate and technically correct. In some cases, reasoning and rationale for certain conclusions may require a detailed explanation. In all cases, the logical development of the consultant's case should be clearly and succinctly presented.

The written report should begin with an executive summary that is no more than one or two pages long. It provides the client with a snapshot of the analysis done, the conclusions reached, and the recommendations offered. Detail and rationale are not possible here. The executive summary captures the client's interest and provides the impetus for digging into the heart of the study.

After the executive summary, the purpose of the consulting project should be detailed. It is a refinement of the statement of work that was developed early in the consulting relationship and notes the areas covered in the report and the basic expectations that the report seeks to

FIGURE 2.1　<u>OUTLINE OF THE FINAL WRITTEN REPORT</u>

    I. Executive summary
   II. Purpose of the consulting project
  III. Methods and procedures
  IV. Findings and recommendations
   V. Implementation
  VI. Appendixes
 VII. Bibliography

meet. This section may also note any constraints that limited the consultant in executing the statement of work.

Next, the report should indicate the methods and procedures used to gather data and to structure the conclusions and recommendations. This section may be detailed but shouldn't ramble. The intent is to demonstrate to the client the thorough and complete nature of the processes used to reach final decisions. Beyond that fundamental perspective, most clients don't care about the details and nuances of the procedures, so they shouldn't take up extensive portions of the report. If particular methodologies need to be detailed, such as the design of the survey instrument or method to derive the sample population, these should be mentioned in the methods section and explained in more detail in appendixes. This allows those who are interested to examine the methods without frustrating the typical reader or taking the focus from the action items of the report.

The main portion of the report presents the findings and recommendations. Both conclusions and their rationales must be carefully and fully developed. As noted earlier, business owners tend to be bottom-line people. Therefore, arguments that demonstrate financial or competitive advantages are particularly effective.

A final section should discuss how recommendations can be implemented. Again, the practical nature of small business owners suggests that they appreciate ideas and thoughts on how recommendations can be effectively put into action.

Appendixes that provide more specific explanations of methods, offer supporting evidence and documentation, and present graphs and exhibits conclude the report. They are often interesting additions that augment and support the report's narrative portions. Finally, a bibliography should be included if appropriate.

Throughout the writing process, every effort should be made to be direct and succinct. The goal is not to create award-winning literature: The purpose is to explain findings and help guide the client to necessary action.

Oral presentation. Consultants should meet with clients to orally summarize the written report and allow for client questions. The oral summation is a chance for consultants to communicate the importance of their recommendations and the potential impact on the business of the recommendations. Consultants shouldn't just read the written report—that's a waste of time—but should present highlights. It's helpful if clients have had a chance to review the written report; and in most situations it's helpful if a visual presentation accompanies the oral presentation. A visual presentation helps consultants better structure the oral presentation and helps clients follow it as well as provides an opportunity to return to previous points if desired.

The oral presentation is also an opportunity for consultants and clients to discuss ideas not included in the report, some of which clients may have recently developed. Possible problems with implementation should be noted, and potential developments in the industry might be discussed.

Finally, consultants should always leave the door open for additional meetings and additional consulting. Repeat business is easier to get than new business. A client who has been happy with a consultant often uses that consultant again. The consulting process began with building rapport, and so it should end in a way that allows the rapport to continue.

DISCUSSION QUESTIONS

1. What are some of the ways consultants can build trust and rapport with clients?
2. Why are clients often reluctant to share sensitive information (such as financials) with consultants? How can consultants help clients to share?
3. What are the key actions consultants need to take to build a meaningful consulting relationship with clients?
4. Highlight the complexities of the problem definition and the data-gathering and analysis stages and indicate steps that help address these complexities.
5. Why is it so important to make sure that the final written report is client focused rather than technically or academically focused?

NOTES

1. Howard Shenson and Ted Nicholas, *The Complete Guide to Consulting Success* (Chicago: Dearborn Financial Publishing, 1993).

Providing Direction for Growth and Change

The definition of an emerging small business in Chapter 1 emphasizes the business's focus on actively pursuing growth. To grow successfully, a business must be involved with the process and dynamics of change. Change can be chaotic, or it can be focused with a clear sense of direction. Vision and mission statements help clarify a business's direction. Therefore, the themes of change, vision, and mission become underpinnings of meaningful strategic planning for new and emerging small businesses. Once you have completed this chapter, you should be able to

- understand the forces for change that affect new and emerging businesses;
- recognize the foundations of resistance to change and apply an approach for managing growth and change;
- recognize the power of innovation and the ways a small business can encourage creativity and innovation;
- understand the value of a vision statement and how to craft a meaningful vision for a business; and

35

- understand the value of a mission statement and be able to develop a mission statement for a business.

A FOCUS ON GROWTH AND CHANGE

Making changes is often one of the most difficult, troubling, and perplexing obstacles that a business encounters. Even in the face of tremendous growth opportunities, implementing change often thwarts a business and its people. Thinking about business growth and change introduces a fundamental dilemma of business life. On one hand, most managers understand that a business that doesn't change will have difficulty surviving in a competitive environment. On the other hand, the process of change is often met with resistance and a strong tendency to maintain the status quo.

Forces for Change

Forces for change surround new and emerging businesses. Some of these forces are clearly recognized; others are more subtle. Consider the case of Terry Precision Bicycles for Women, a business started by Georgena Terry, a biking enthusiast and Xerox employee. Terry was convinced that the high-quality road bikes on the market were designed for men, causing discomfort and pain by forcing women to bend over farther than normal. In response, Terry designed a custom bike frame for women that shortened the distance between the seat and handlebars. Terry Precision Bicycles for Women seemed to tap an unmet need in the market, and its high-quality bikes, selling from $600 to $1600, experienced strong initial success.

Terry did a number of things right. First, it had a clear understanding of the nature of bicycle customers and what they needed in their products. Second, careful research of the competition was performed that found current products didn't address the needs of female bikers. Third, it developed and marketed a product that addressed a market niche broad enough to provide meaningful revenue and profits. Although this initial picture appears to capture the essence of small business success, that success will be short-lived unless there is a proper posture toward change.

Terry's continued growth depends on recognizing the forces for change:

- Response of competitors
- Proliferation of technology
- Rising and shifting customer demands
- Push for improved products and services
- Economic trends
- Drive for quality and efficiency
- Changing rules and regulations
- New and unexpected crisis

One of the most powerful forces for change is the response of competitors. For example, Terry's competitors, such as Trek and Cannondale, are large and well established. Are these competitors likely to produce competing models? Will they present an advertising blitz to convince customers that Terry's product is not really unique? Terry is prompted to change because the competition is unlikely to stand still. Further, customers are likely to expect more products and more improvements. Resting on past laurels is not a long-term option. Interestingly, Terry has accepted the challenge of change. It recognized that many of its customers' concerns centered on the need to make the bike saddle or seat more comfortable for women. Accordingly, Terry designed a new seat with a shorter nose that better fits a woman's body. This change, prompted by new customer demands, is an apparent winner. Today, seats account for about 30 percent of Terry's business.[1]

Building an Environment of Creativity and Innovation

The forces of change suggest that an emerging business should always be poised for change. Creativity and innovation must be watchwords and guiding themes. And even though they go hand-in-hand, creativity and innovation are not the same. Creativity is a process that involves new and different patterns of thinking and behaving. Innovation is the result of those creative activities. In simplest terms, creativity leads to innovation. The emerging business needs to create an environment or culture that encourages creativity and innovation and views change as a key foundation for continued business success. Let's look at some things a manager can do to foster such an environment.

Staying in touch with customers.   One of the best ways to stay on the edge of creativity and innovation is to stay in close contact with customers and those you would like to have as customers. If managers pay careful attention, customers will often signal changes, improvements, and innovations that are needed. Further, customers will also signal areas of growth where meaningful business opportunities may exist.

Investing in training and development.   There may be no better engine for creativity and innovation than the training and development activities of the business—an area many small business managers avoid. Often, managers reason that training is expensive and that limited resources are best committed to more obvious, bottom-line activities. Buying a new machine, purchasing a new software program, or repairing a press takes precedence over funds committed to the training and development of people. Clearly, trade-offs are always involved, but training exposes employees to new ideas, new ways of thinking, and new options for the business. It acquaints them with approaches that have worked for others. Many times, training is fertile ground for the development of ideas and innovations that help the business position itself for growth. Jere Stead, former chairman of Square D and Legent Corporation, once said that if he had $1 to spend, he would spend it on training. From training comes the insights needed to survive and grow.

Challenging existing procedures and routines.   Managers of emerging businesses must be willing to challenge existing procedures and routines, a particularly difficult action because most procedures were originally initiated to help the business. Accordingly, it can be hard to recognize that procedures that made sense in the past are now unnecessarily constraining or restricting the business as it grows. For example, a small business's requirement of top management approval for expenditures can help ensure cost containment and build a culture of careful attention to financial control. Yet this same approach can slow decision making and frustrate skilled managers as the business grows and responds to its markets.

Unfortunately, procedures and routines breed a life of their own. Often, we stick with them simply because "that's the way we've always done it." Our rule of thumb is to challenge existing routines, subjecting them to a bottom-line litmus test. Namely, managers must ask, "Does this rule, policy, procedure, or routine help the business as it grows?" If the question doesn't receive a solid affirmative response, careful reconsideration of the routine should be taken.

Encouraging risk taking.   Managers should encourage their people to be active risk takers. Recognize what this statement says and, more important, what it does not say. Risk taking doesn't involve wild, off-the-cuff whimsical movements with a gut-level feel that they make sense and will prove to be business winners. Risk taking is careful and deliberate. It requires study and examination. Yet it recognizes that there are no certainties in growing markets. At some point, the business must step forward and make its best, well-calculated decision, even though that decision is wrought with uncertainty and risk.

Leaders must encourage their people to know the business landscape, to know their competitors, and to study and strategize. But they must also encourage their people to think beyond traditional answers and take calculated risks. Whether such encouragement is merely espoused or is actually practiced can be measured by how mistakes are handled.

Accepting and learning from mistakes. Many managers pay lip service to risk taking. It is a popular and trendy value for managers to espouse. Unfortunately, many of these same managers, through their condemnation and punishment of failed risks, are able to drive creative risk taking from their business. Risk taking, from time to time, will lead to missteps and mistakes; sometimes, even well thought out and carefully considered decisions are unsuccessful. The market suddenly changes. The economy takes a sudden and unexpected dip. Consumers demonstrate a shift in their expectations and preferences. And sometimes failure is the outcome of risk taking.

Innovative managers understand the dynamic of risk taking. They recognize that mistakes will occur but, more important, they view mistakes as natural byproducts of creativity. Mistakes are to be dissected. They should be avenues of learning to avoid future occurrences. However, as long as risks are taken and uncertainty remains, mistakes will occur.

A classic story will illustrate our point. Many years ago, a young manager was called to the office of IBM founder Tom Watson. The young manager had misread a risky venture. Although he had carefully studied and prepared, the strategies he proposed failed in the uncertain and dynamic information technology environment. He could have played it safe, but he took a calculated risk that cost the company over $10 million! Sitting in Watson's office, the young manager fidgeted nervously and offered his resignation. Watson's response was quick and decisive: "You can't be serious. We've just spent $10 million educating you."[2] Watson's message and its impact are clear. Mistakes are part of ongoing learning in a creative environment.

Encouraging a diversity of opinions. First, innovative businesses genuinely encourage divergent viewpoints and perspectives, often achieved through balanced, representative teams. No one necessarily likes or feels comfortable with the person who always seems to take a different spin on a topic or issue, the devil's advocate. Few people actively embrace the employee who always seems to challenge conventional approaches and asks "what if" questions. Yet employees like this demonstrate precisely the diversity that must be present. Diversity of ideas is the springboard of creativity.

Second, diversity has meaning only if diverse views are actively considered, thoroughly pondered, and conscientiously weighed. The temptation must be fought to dismiss differing opinions just because they *are* different—easier said than done. It falls largely on management's shoulders to demonstrate a respectful and positive approach toward diversity in order to unleash its creative potential for a business.

Sometimes, one of the best ways for an emerging business to ensure diversity of views, background, and talents is to hire people with skills that are missing from the business mix. Often, founders recognize that while their novel ideas initially propelled the business, they don't have the background to build an emerging business. They may need people on their team with richer management experiences. It takes strength of leadership to admit such gaps, take action to fill such needs, and heed the advice of new managers. For example, everyone marvels at the creative energies of the youthful founders of Yahoo!, Jerry Yang and David Filo. Yang and Filo recognized early opportunities as Internet use was beginning to grow. Yet these company founders were astute enough to bring on board more seasoned managers who developed many of the strategies that led to the business's phenomenal growth and success. Hiring Timothy Koogle as CEO and Jeffrey Mallett as COO brought new approaches, such as upbeat marketing campaigns and charging fees to advertisers. The new managers helped transform Yahoo! from a basic Internet directory into a pivotal hub of Internet activity.[3]

Foundations of Resistance

Resistance to change refers here to the tendency of people in a business to maintain the status quo and keep things the way they are. Even well thought out and logical change is often met with resistance. Why is this so? The status quo represents stability and consistency. For many people, dealing with what is known provides a sense of security. Change implies uncertainty and risk. People are always wondering if they will be better or worse off as a result of change. Accordingly, there is considerable stress that often accompanies change.

People who resist change are not bizarre or aberrant. In fact, people tend to resist change for such logical and understandable reasons, as

- not being convinced of the need for change;
- not wanting to lose something of value;
- not understanding the implications and assuming the worst;
- fear of failure or lessened effectiveness; and
- a low tolerance for change.

Many people resist change simply because they are not convinced change is needed. They may argue that the business is doing fine right now and that it doesn't make sense to change what is already working. Others resist change because they are afraid they will lose something of value, such as their current position, job status, power within the current business system, or even job security. Some people resist change because they don't understand where the change is taking the business and what its outcomes and implications will be. Often, they make extreme assumptions about the negative impacts of change because they lack evidence to the contrary. Some people resist change because they are afraid they will fail or be less effective under the new system than they are now. This, too, is understandable. Interestingly, this fear afflicts a range of people, even those who are quite skilled and talented. Finally, some people simply have a low tolerance for change. Their personality prefers the structure and order that is destroyed by change and is therefore uncomfortable.

Because most resistance revolves around fear and misunderstanding, managers who wish to initiate changes should attempt to provide clear direction and communication and deal with underlying fears.

Managing for Growth and Change

The preceding discussion has stressed the value and necessity of change, the impact of creativity and innovation within the change process, and the power of resistance to change that must be recognized and addressed. It is the responsibility of managers to help their business move through resistance to embrace growth and change. No magical steps exist, but managers of emerging businesses should keep in mind four recommendations.

First, managers must explain the need for change. As noted earlier, this need may be clear because the forces for change are so strong: The competition may be threatening market share or new technology is demanding a more efficient approach. In such cases, the bottom line may be so imperiled that owners and employees know a crisis is looming, and the need for change is clear. However, the emerging business may face a different scenario: Business may be booming, new market opportunities may be apparent, and employees and owners may be experiencing positive results. It can be difficult to explain the need for change under such conditions. Forward thinking, proactive change may be tough to sell. Yet that is exactly the manager's job. By using existing evidence and logical projections, a manager must demonstrate the need for change so convincingly that the broad majority of the company's employees recognize its necessity.

Once the need for change is established, a second recommended step becomes critical. Managers and other key leaders must provide a vision of the change. (The vision statement is significant within the change process and is explained in detail shortly.) The vision must be clear and convincing enough that it provides everyone in the business with a mental picture of what the process of change can yield. If the vision makes sense, the logic and buy-in for change is enhanced.

The third recommended step is for managers to listen to and address the resistance that will naturally accompany any proposed change. Remember, resistance is not a bad response; it is a response born of uncertainty, confusion, and fear. Therefore, communication is a key. Fears should be addressed. Clarifications should be offered. New expectations should be presented. Managers should listen to the reasons for resistance and respond as directly and honestly as they can. They should show employees both the organizational and personal benefits of the change. Managers should explain where and how employees fit in the new scheme of activities. Getting employees actively involved in planning and working through the details of a change can be an excellent approach for gaining needed input and acceptance. As a general rule, people feel better about change when there is open, involved, and continual communication.

Finally, managers should develop a plan for change. People are more accepting of change when they believe there is a logical, well thought out process of planned change in place. In many ways, this is one of the key values that a good strategic plan can help provide.

SETTING A DIRECTION FOR GROWTH AND CHANGE

Some managers tend to write off or deemphasize establishing a direction for change in the strategic planning process, telling themselves that they already know where the firm is headed. But vision and mission are among the most important considerations in the planning process. A firm's vision and mission statements provide focus. Without such statements, the company may flounder, headed in no particular direction. The resulting confusion may not only stifle the progress of the business but it may frustrate and demoralize employees.

Providing a Vision for the Business

Often, small business leaders and entrepreneurs are visionaries. Sam Walton of Wal-Mart, J. W. Marriott of Marriott Hotels, Paul Galvin of Motorola, and Michael Dell of Dell Computers each started small businesses, but each had a vision for a new product, service, or method of distribution. Their vision became the unifying force for their respective organizations.

Vision is a necessary ingredient for emerging businesses. As the business environment becomes more and more complex, it is necessary for businesses to focus on the future so they will continue to meet the needs of an ever changing customer.

The vision statement.   The vision statement is a comment on the desirable and possible future state that a business will strive to attain. It should be crisp, clear, brief, and meaningful—not a set of platitudes. It should be unique to the particular business, and it should excite and energize people about the business and where it's headed. Such visions can be as straightforward as the one John Kennedy set for the U.S. space program in the early days of his administration—a man on the moon by the end of the decade. It can be fundamental yet offer clear direction and intent. Although certainly not a small business, General Electric states its vision as being either number one or number two in every business it's in. An emerging business may have similar visions. For example, a small but rapidly growing optical firm established the vision of becoming "Number 1 in customer recognition and choice in our region within three years." Or consider the visionary comment that Boston Beer Company includes as part of its company philosophy: "We are committed to making Samuel Adams the largest and most respected craft or imported beer in the United States before 2006." Remember that visions need to be broad, yet clearly offer direction and focus for the business efforts of the firm.

Development of the company's vision. Some may believe in a popular myth that business leaders are prone to have periodic flashes of brilliance, bringing them clear and inspirational business visions. While such revelations may occur on occasion, they are far from the norm. In most cases, leaders evolve their business visions through careful study and thorough understanding of their business and their competition, and by actively involving and listening to key constituents. Talking to customers, talking with employees, and questioning suppliers and vendors can all breed the kinds of perspectives needed to build meaningful visions. Straightforward inquiries such as asking customers "What would you like to see in a business like ours?" or "How can we better serve you and your needs?" can provide key perspectives.

Communicating the vision. If the vision is to have any meaningful impact, it must be communicated clearly to the employees who will share and work toward its success. Most people argue that the leaders of the business must be the "lead spokespersons" of the vision. Essentially, this means that leaders must show why the vision makes sense and is necessary. Leaders may have to win sentiment for the vision. They may have to display confidence and enthusiasm for the vision—actually a response to resistance to change. The goal of communicating the vision is to help secure buy-in for the vision among all those affected by it. This includes helping people see that they have some part of the vision and that they have a place in the business as it emerges and changes. Through such a process of careful communication, the vision can become an underlying force or theme that guides business thinking and action.

Providing a Mission for the Business

Although the vision establishes a general directional tone for the business, it provides no detail or precision. For example, the optical business noted above established the vision of being the customer's first choice but said nothing about how it intended to proceed to meet this vision. It is the mission that addresses some of the questions that the vision, by virtue of its thematic and inspirational tone, cannot. The mission begins to focus and expresses additional precision.

The mission statement. The mission statement is a concise statement of the general nature and direction of the company. By carefully delineating the underlying aim, scope, and direction of the business, the mission statement becomes an outline of what the company will do and what it will be. Although the mission statement is purposely broad, it must offer a clear word picture of the firm. Often, an elaborate-sounding, sweeping compilation of platitudes is offered as a mission statement. Such a statement fails to provide the precision and scope necessary to be useful as a meaningful planning tool. The owner should ask, "What separates us from similar companies?" The answer becomes a unique mission statement that is the basis for a definitive business strategy.

The value of the mission statement. A written mission statement has two major values. The first is as a communication both inside and outside the firm. Naturally, the financial community will be interested in the direction the company is moving. But perhaps more important is internal communication. Often, employees complain that they never know what is happening. They don't know what management's plans are or how they, the employees, fit within those plans, which makes it difficult for them to be committed and motivated workers. The mission statement helps clarify the firm's vision and the employees' role in it.

The second major value is the commitment that the owner of the firm has to the mission once it is printed and publicized. If a concept or philosophy is believed strongly enough to put in writing, then everyone affected can expect that the idea will be followed. It's like New Year's resolutions, but with higher stakes. If you make resolutions but tell no one, there is no particular incentive to keep them. But if you write them down, ponder them, type them up, post them on the refrigerator, tell your friends about them, maybe even wager that you will keep them, this public commitment means you can't break them without losing face (or maybe money). In the same way, the written mission statement commits the manager to the stated strategy and philosophy and may result in equal commitment by others in and around the business. Such a commitment in no way suggests that a company's mission is cast in stone, never to be altered. Mission statements, as representations of the firm's place in a dynamic environment, may change over time. However, such changes evolve as the firm assesses movements in its competitive situation. The mission statement provides a central focus and unifying drive for the business within its planning horizon.

The first part of a mission statement. The mission statement contains two major elements. Each should be given careful consideration.

The first element of the mission statement defines and clearly specifies the basic *nature of the business.* Four different areas must be considered:

1. The industry and product line of the company and the type of services provided
2. The firm's position in the distribution channel (Is the company a wholesaler, a manufacturer, a retailer, or a mail-order business?)
3. The prime goals of the firm (quality, breadth of product line, price, or service)
4. The target market (Who does the firm presently serve? Who does it intend to serve in the relevant future?)

By telling explicitly what the firm is, the mission statement also tells implicitly what the firm is not. These limiting statements serve as a control to keep the general direction intact, similar to fences on either side of a highway. Consider the following example.

A woman decides to open a bicycle shop that sells and services bicycles. After a few months, she is offered the opportunity to add a line of mopeds. Reasoning that mopeds are simply bicycles with a small motor, she adds the line. Later, the regional manager for Honda motorcycles stops by. The local Honda dealer is retiring, and this presents the shop owner a once-in-a-lifetime opportunity to land a coveted Honda dealership. Now she has a bicycle/moped/motorcycle business. Somewhat later, the entrepreneur is presented the opportunity to take on a line of snowmobiles. Reasoning that snowmobiles really have much in common with motorcycles except that they run primarily on skis instead of wheels, she adds this line too. The story could continue indefinitely as the woman adds garden tractors, lawnmowers, snowblowers, and so on. The point is that the one-time bicycle shop has become a highly diversified dealership for a number of slightly related products. In the process, the owner has overextended herself, is no longer able to do anything well, and has incurred substantial debt—in short, she has lost control of her operation. A well-written and closely observed mission statement would allow the owner to specialize in bicycles until she decided it was time to expand. Then she could carefully evaluate the market and her financial ability to take on an added line. Lines would be added at a controlled rate and with adequate financing.

Many businesses, large and small, fail because of rapid, uncontrolled growth. For example, large businesses often acquire unrelated firms or start new businesses in unrelated areas with the stated goal of broadening their earnings base or gaining a countercyclical business. Many of these same subsidiaries are later divested as the parent firm's executives decide to "return to the things we do best." Obviously the corporation's management strayed from its basic mission and later realized its error.

The second part of a mission statement. The second major element of the mission statement is an expression of the firm's *management philosophy and underlying values.* Even though the mission statement by itself cannot create an organizational culture, it does define and espouse the kind of culture the owner wants. Over the past dozen years, much has been written about "corporate culture" and its impact, power, and influence on the behavior and activities of large organizations. The concept of culture is equally important for the small firm. The mission statement should capture the owner's basic philosophy of how business will be conducted. In simplest terms, the mission statement should explain the core values that are most central and most critical to the business. The result is a value orientation that becomes an important guide for subsequent management action.

For example, a small manufacturer included in its mission statement the phrase, "We build quality into every product we produce." The owner wanted to convey clearly to all customers and potential customers that the business was committed to the highest level of quality assurance. The owner emphasized the significance of this theme by including the phrase as the company motto on its business letterhead.

In making a philosophical or cultural declaration, the mission statement may say a great deal about the firm. Will the firm be a risk taker? Will it be employee oriented? Will the firm be run according to the highest ethical standards? Will it be an aggressive competitor? Will it be a pioneer or a follower, a me-too firm? The key is to include those items about which management feels strongly and omit those items about which it does not. For example, the mission statement may mention nothing about a promote-from-within policy and instead discuss the strategy of hiring young managers with new ideas.

Increasingly, owners of small and emerging businesses are recognizing that while the formulation of the company mission is ultimately their responsibility, the process need not be an isolated activity. In fact, the formulation of a mission rarely comes from a flash of owner insight or inspiration. More typically, owners engage in a development process that involves input from numerous sources representing a range of stakeholders, including suppliers, customers, and employees. Owners should recognize the significance and value of stakeholder input. In particular, employees at all levels often have important views and help guide and foster the mission's tone and direction.

Guidelines for Mission Statements

Jones and Kahaner, in their excellent look at some of the best mission statements in the United States today, highlight a key starting rule or guideline: Keep the statement simple.[4] Simple doesn't always mean short, but it does always mean simple. Clarity and directness must be emphasized. Some businesses, such as Lowe's, are quite succinct. "Lowe's is in the business of providing products to help customers build, improve, and enjoy their homes. Our goal is to out-service the competition and be our customers' 1st Choice Store for these products."[5]

Further, the style or tone of the writing should reflect the philosophy of the business. Look at the example of the Joy Toy Company in Figure 3.1. You really get a sense of the business through the statement and the manner in which it is communicated. In this way, the mission communicates some of the subtle flavor of the business and its unique character.

Finally, be sure to have broad involvement in developing the mission. The mission will mean more and have a far greater motivational impact if those in the organization feel they have had a hand in crafting it.

Sample mission statements. Figure 3.1 is a mission statement for a small toy-manufacturing company. The statement clearly lays out the nature of the firm as well as the tone or philosophy of the company. At the same time it does not give away any proprietary secrets. Figure 3.2 provides examples of other companies' mission statements.

In sum, the mission statement must do only two things, but it must do them well. First, it must set forth the direction of the business, thereby specifying what the business is and what it is not. Second, it must set forth the tone or culture of the business based on the owner's philosophy of how the business should be run.

FIGURE 3.1 <u>JOY'S TOY COMPANY MISSION STATEMENT</u>

Joy's Toy Company produces a wide line of moderately priced educational toys for preschool and young school-age children. We service a four-state area surrounding Missouri and sell directly to schools or school district buying centers.

We care about children and view their education as the critical part of our task. Our toys are designed to enrich the child's educational experience. All design work is done in-house to assure responsive, innovative products.

Our first product priority is quality. We would rather lose a sale by being overpriced than sell low-quality merchandise. We offer quick and accessible service and repair on all merchandise we sell.

In hiring sales representatives, we seek to attract former primary school teachers who are in tune with the needs and wants of children and who can identify with the concerns of parents. We exclusively promote from within.

THE CONSULTANT'S VIEWPOINT

The themes of this chapter present some important challenges for the consultant. While we have built the case for organizational change, we have clearly noted the difficulty and resistance that is associated with such change. A consultant must recognize that most business managers understand and accept the value of change. Indeed, enlightened managers of emerging businesses usually recognize that change is essential to survival. They know that their business must be poised for change if they are to be successful in a dynamic competitive environment. In short, at least at an intellectual level, they probably know and accept the necessity of change. However, the consultant must exercise care. Managers' intellectual recognition of the value and necessity of change does not ensure their acceptance and willingness to embrace change. Often, at the gut level change represents upheaval. Accordingly, managers are reluctant to take the steps toward change that they know make sense and are needed. While this may appear puzzling or even illogical, it is a reality the consultant often encounters.

The seasoned consultant recognizes managers' reluctance to change and must address clients "where they are" rather than "where they should be" or "where we would hope they would be." Therefore, the first thing a consultant must do is sense whether there is a readiness for

FIGURE 3.2   SAMPLE MISSION STATEMENTS

Blazing Graphics

Blazing Graphics will provide you with the most effective visual communication available. We will help you achieve all of your goals while providing you with the greatest value both seen and unseen.

Here at Blazing Graphics we take the time to do things right. We do this by controlling the entire graphic arts process. This enables us to better coordinate each job while providing a higher level of service.

Our mission is to ensure exceptional quality by opening up communication between crafts normally separated and at times adverse to one another.

Here at Blazing Graphics we have committed ourselves and our resources to being on the forefront of technology.

Creative technical know-how is the single most critical determinant of economic competitiveness.

It's our belief that together we can create an environment that will be both personally and professionally fulfilling for all the people who make up the Blazing Community.

Source: Sharon Nelton, "Put Your Purpose in Writing," *Nation's Business,* 82 (February 1994), 61–64.

Cascade Properties

Cascade Properties provides services for residential and commercial real estate sales. In addition, we have a property management firm that markets apartments, residential homes, office buildings, and commercial complexes. We are also involved in the environmental services area.

As the real estate industry continues to change, we will aggressively explore new market opportunities and continually educate our associates to provide outstanding service to our clients and customers.

Source: Company documents

Celestial Seasonings

Our mission is to grow and dominate the U.S. specialty tea market by exceeding consumer expectations with:

The best tasting, 100 percent natural hot and iced teas, packaged with celestial art and philosophy, creating the most valued tea experience.

Through leadership, innovation, focus, and teamwork we are dedicated to continuously improving value to our consumers, customers, employees, and stakeholders with a quality-first organization.

Source: Patricia Jones and Larry Kahaner, *Say It and Live It: The 50 Corporate Mission Statements That Hit the Mark* (New York: Currency, 1995), p. 53.

Bard Optical

Bard Optical provides the latest technological advances in vision care to meet the optometric needs of the retail consumer by providing the lowest possible price and highest quality service, while maintaining a reasonable profit.

Source: Company documents

change within the business. Readiness exists when participants in a business understand that the need for change is so strong that they must proceed along the course of change. They must understand that failure to change is an unacceptable alternative. The consultant must help the business's leaders and managers see why change is essential. Often, looking at competitor moves and bottom-line impacts provide persuasive evidence that change must occur. The trick is for the consultant to build the state of readiness before the business is faced with a bottom-line crisis.

Readiness starts at the top, but it must include the bulk of the business's employees. We suggest that a critical mass of the employees should be helped to recognize the fundamental need for change before progressing along the path of planned change. If this underlying readiness fails to materialize, any change action is on shaky foundation. The consultant helps build the broad support needed to convince employees of the need for change.

Of course, readiness is only part of the issue. Establishing a meaningful vision and mission is also important. Recognize the logic of the order here. Providing a new vision and mission without a fundamental attention to readiness is risky. Even with readiness ensured, however, the direction of change—as noted through the vision and mission—must be clear. The consultant must play a lead role here but be careful that the evolving vision and mission come from the participants in the business. The consultant should facilitate the crafting of a vision and mission for a business; the consultant should not create them.

To facilitate the development and crafting of the mission statement, the consultant should try to guide the company's managers to critically evaluate the business from an external or outside perspective. Rather than using an internal focus (considering what types of products/services the company offers), the consultant should encourage managers to focus on who the customer is, the types of needs the company satisfies, and how the company satisfies those needs. By focusing on these three areas, the consultant can ensure that the company will be using an external perspective to develop its mission statement. Too often a company will define its business simply by the products/services it offers. This internal approach usually provides too narrow a definition for the mission statement.

Finally, the consultant should be prepared to allow considerable time for the final mission statement to evolve. It may take several iterations before the company is satisfied with the semantics of its mission statement. It can become a tedious process in which each word is analyzed and critiqued. This is perfectly acceptable. It is critical that the company is satisfied with each word because others will use the mission statement to guide them in developing future strategic plans.

DISCUSSION QUESTIONS

1. Why is the process of change so difficult for emerging small businesses?
2. What are some of the attitudes and actions that managers of emerging businesses can encourage to build a climate of creativity and innovation?
3. Why is the mission statement so important for emerging small businesses?
4. What are the parts of the mission statement?
5. Is it easy to identify a company's management philosophy? Can you gain a sense of it by visiting the business? Could you determine the philosophy by interviewing some of the key managers of the business?
6. Select an emerging small business in your community and obtain a copy of its mission statement. Does it portray the information that has been noted in this chapter?

NOTES

1. Gary Fallesen, "Women's Point of View," www.rochesterdandc. com/rec/biking/rb7087a.html, accessed May 28, 1997.

2. Warren Bennis and Burt Nanus, *Leaders: The Strategies for Taking Charge* (New York: Harper & Row, 1985), p. 76.

3. Kara Swisher, "The Two Grown-Ups Behind Yahoo!'s Surge," *The Wall Street Journal,* April 10, 1998, B1,B5.

4. Patricia Jones and Larry Kahaner, *Say It and Live It: The 50 Corporate Mission Statements That Hit the Mark* (New York: Currency, 1995), pp. 263–67.

5. Ibid., p. 157.

CHAPTER 4

ENVIRONMENTAL ANALYSIS— GENERAL ENVIRONMENT

New and emerging businesses are affected by the environment in which they operate. Such factors as economic conditions, government regulation, changing customer buying behavior, technological enhancements, and competition may impact business performance. As an important step in the planning process, environmental analyses are performed to identify and assess external factors that can potentially impact the future of an organization. After reading this chapter you should be able to

- understand the significance of external analysis;
- recognize why managers of emerging firms must be proactive;
- realize the importance of establishing an external frame of reference for strategic planning; and
- identify the impact of general environmental factors on industry performance.

THE VALUE OF ENVIRONMENTAL ANALYSIS

Planning in today's dynamic environment may be the single most significant factor affecting a company's success or failure. New and emerging businesses must be particularly sensitive to environmental influences for three important reasons.

First, an emerging firm's responsiveness to environmental issues may be a source of considerable competitive strength. A new or emerging business can stay closer to the consumer than larger businesses can. By virtue of its smaller size, an emerging firm can move with speed, flexibility, and sensitivity to accommodate shifts in customer preferences. Larger, more structured, and hierarchically bound organizations may be unable to alter their direction or focus quickly. Consequently, a new or emerging business may be able to etch out a competitive edge against large firms.

Second, emerging businesses are particularly vulnerable to environmental influences. They cannot afford to misread their environment. Although one mistake or one misreading of a critical environmental trend may affect a large firm adversely, the error can usually be easily absorbed into the breadth of its total operations. However, a similar mistake may destroy a small business. Rare is the small business whose resources can withstand such mistakes.

Third, emerging firms usually don't have the resources needed to alter their environment; rather, they must respond to environmental changes. Therefore, it is imperative that managers of emerging firms understand what is currently happening in its environment. In addition, they must understand how that environment is changing, thus making it necessary for them to recognize the major drivers that will affect the future of the industry.

Industry drivers are factors that shape the future of an industry in terms of both demand and competition. Managers of successful firms, large or small, have a good understanding of what drives their industries. For example, is the industry driven by government regulation? Is it driven by technological change? Is it driven by increasing needs for quality products? Is it driven by the imperative to control costs and offer products at lower prices? Is the industry affected by changing demographics? Obviously, there can be many environmental drivers. It is therefore necessary for successful managers to be able to identify key drivers in their respective industries.

The three reasons noted above—the benefits of small size, vulnerability to competition, and the need to identify changes in the industry—

underscore the need for environmental analysis. A thorough environmental analysis is the difference between a proactive and reactive business.

PROACTIVE MANAGEMENT

One of the themes of this book is that planning stems from a proactive perspective. Simply stated, proactive managers look to the future and anticipate and plan for change. One reason for emphasizing environmental analysis so strongly is that it helps the business develop a proactive rather than reactive style of management. Proactive managers see opportunities on the horizon and position the business to benefit from them. They also recognize impending threats and take actions to overcome them before disaster strikes.

A reactive business, however, is driven by day-to-day demands: Events occur and the firm responds. A reactive business is always undergoing a new, usually unanticipated trauma. Crisis management is the evolving style of operation and putting out the largest fire is the focus of activities. In all likelihood, the business that fails to recognize and analyze its environment will become the victim of changes and forces within that environment. The literature on small business failures is filled with examples.

An example of proactive thinking is featured in Profile 4.1. Andrew and Thomas Parkinson took advantage of two significant environmental trends—the increasing use of home computers featuring online services and the decrease in leisure time among contemporary families. They capitalized on both trends to provide a service for those whose time is perhaps more precious than money.

THE NATURE OF ENVIRONMENTAL ANALYSIS

A company's environment establishes the context within which the company functions. The environment contains a set of factors that affect the business and its performance but that are external to and largely beyond its control. When managers perform an environmental analysis, they identify and examine key external factors and assess and evaluate the impact these factors will likely have on a firm's operations and suc-

PROFILE 4.1

PEAPOD, INC.

In select Jewel Food Stores in Chicago and Safeway, Inc., stores in San Francisco, some people are shopping carefully even though not for themselves. They are employees of Peapod, Inc., a computerized shopping service. Founders Andrew and Thomas Parkinson have made the idea of grocery shopping via computer a reality for over 7,000 customers.

Peapod's customers use their home computers to "shop" for groceries. They are able to select specific brands, compare prices, browse electronic "aisles," such as cereal and breakfast or ethnic foods, to get ideas, and even use coupons. The software, which is the key to the operation, also allows customers to maintain grocery lists and indicate acceptable substitutes if the store is out of stock on a particular item. The orders are then transmitted via computer, telephone, or fax to Peapod's professional shoppers. The shoppers gather the groceries, which are delivered within a 90-minute window. Customers can pay by check, credit card, or computer account. Customers subscribe to the service either on a flat rate or per-usage basis.

Sales in 1997 increased by 104 percent to $29.2 million, and Peapod plans to introduce a new generation of online shopping software in 1998. All of this is possible because two entrepreneurs found a way to combine technology with one of the most mundane of all tasks—shopping for groceries.

Source: www.peapod.com, accessed May 22, 1998.

cess. Managers analyze present forces and also attempt to project trends and anticipate changes. Environmental analysis is future oriented—managers seek to determine what problems and opportunities will likely be created by changes in the environment.

FIGURE 4.1   <u>ENVIRONMENTAL ANALYSIS</u>

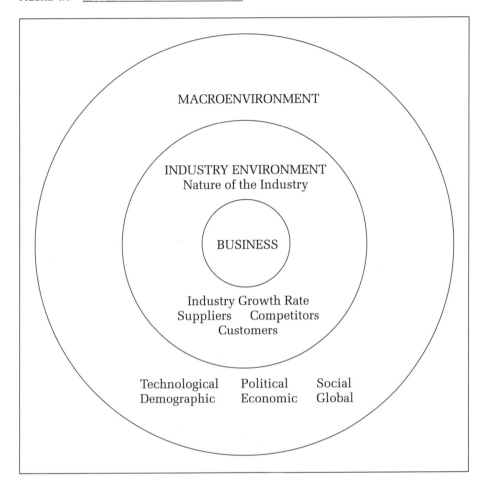

The process of analyzing the environment is illustrated schematically in Figure 4.1. The broadest set of variables comprise those technological, political/legal, social, demographic, economic, and global variables that may affect the business in only a general way. These variables make up the general or macroenvironment. A somewhat narrower set of variables that may have a more specific impact make up the industry environment. All of these variables tell us something about the dynamics of the industry and the players within it.

ANALYZING THE GENERAL ENVIRONMENT

In this chapter we restrict the firm's external analysis to the macroenvironment; industry and competitive factors are discussed in Chapter 5. The general or macroenvironment comprises variables that are not company or industry specific but apply to and affect all firms, although their impact may be felt differently by each firm. Six areas of macroenvironmental variables need to be considered: technological changes, political and legal changes, social changes, demographic changes, economic changes, and global changes.

Technological Changes

The presence and continued proliferation of computerized information is revolutionizing products, processes, and communications. Companies can now use flexible manufacturing systems to make customized products while simultaneously minimizing costs. Information management is becoming a source of competitive advantage in many industries. It was estimated that in 1997 there were 50 million Internet users worldwide and major service providers reported an average annual growth rate of 150 percent.

New technical processes are rapidly emerging and changing the nature and focus of organizational action. Key technological changes affecting a business and its industry should always be tracked. By following developments reported in trade literature, searching the Internet, and following reports of advances noted by suppliers or sales representatives, business managers may be reasonably aware of these key changes. Failure to monitor and address major technological innovations may adversely affect a firm's competitive position, particularly if competing firms use technical improvements.

Adopting technical improvements does not, of course, mean that every fad or innovation must be accepted. Rather, a careful analysis and systematic consideration of each advance is necessary to determine the potential effect on the firm, thus allowing the best and most relevant changes to be exploited. Further, a manager may avoid being caught in a position where customers perceive the business as being technologically backward or inferior to its competitors. If this occurs, a significant number of customers may be lost, and the business may be forced to incur substantial expense to bring its technology up-to-date and online.

A few years ago, an insightful middle-aged man started his own graphic design business. He had extensive experience in the industry, having been employed by his largest competitor for 14 years. Through his experience and exposure to the industry and his careful analysis of evolving trends, he concluded that all six firms in his selected target market were using outdated equipment and approaches. He felt that his business, by availing itself of the latest technological advances, could offer customers better quality at lower prices, thus attaining a competitive edge. He obviously was right. Today, all of his competitors are using cutting edge software and other technology. The entrepreneur had gained a competitive edge by recognizing the trend and was able to capitalize on that edge for a period of time, which allowed him to gain a foothold in the market in spite of substantial competition.

Political and Legal Changes

Factors such as changes in government policy and regulations, legal developments, and changes in political philosophy may all affect a business. These changes can occur at the federal, state, and local level. It is not unusual for social pressures to prompt enactment of legislative guidelines and requirements that affect small business operations. For example, attempts to change health care policy may have a dramatic effect on both emerging companies' opportunities and their ability to compete.

From time to time, tax laws change, with resulting effects on the structure and reporting practices of new or emerging businesses. Political pressures within a particular community or trade area may affect not only the general business climate but also philosophies toward the promotion of new and emerging businesses. Managers must address these and any number of other political/legal concerns.

Pending judicial decisions that may impact a business should also be monitored closely. For example, deregulation in the airline, trucking, and banking industries has created tremendous growth opportunities for some emerging businesses while threatening the future success of others. Recent deregulation of the utility industry will no doubt create the opportunity for emerging businesses to compete in markets that had been previously reserved for only very large organizations.

Local newspapers, chamber of commerce reports, trade publications, and general business publications (such as *Business Week* and *The Wall Street Journal*) are important informational sources. Even more current information can be found through the many sources available on the Internet. Some computer users make a habit of checking the latest developments each morning. By reading and staying up-to-date on current and impending developments, managers can maintain a reasonably accurate appraisal of political and legal trends and gain enough information to seek out appropriate professionals for more specific guidance when necessary.

Social Changes

Social factors are identified as the general attitudes, preferences, tastes, and beliefs of a society. Two of the most visible social changes in the past couple of decades are health consciousness and environmentalism, two social trends that have influenced numerous industries. The fast-food industry, for example, has responded to health consciousness by offering healthier alternatives such as low-fat sandwiches and salads and has responded to environmentalists by packaging food in biodegradable materials rather than Styrofoam.

Even though social changes have threatened some industries, they have virtually created new industries. With an increase in overall health consciousness, demand for access to a local businessman's small health club increased. The businessman expanded his hours and shortly thereafter expanded his facilities to meet increasing demand. Realizing that his health-conscious patrons were just as concerned with maintaining a healthy diet as they were with exercise, he began to sell a limited line of health food snacks at his club and demand grew considerably. Nonmembers of the club asked if they too could purchase the health food items, citing that his selection was better than that of any of the local grocery stores. Ultimately, he decided to open his own health food store. Rather than focusing on vitamins and supplements, his product line was similar to a traditional grocery store, although his products were all natural. He sold everything from organic milk (milk processed from cows that were not given the bovine growth hormone) to high-fiber pastas. By responding to the social trend of health consciousness, revenues from his all-natural grocery store quickly surpassed revenues from his health club.

As another example, a store catering to runners carried only running shoes 15 years ago and targeted hard-core, serious runners. However, changing social values have twice forced the store to change. Beginning in the mid-1980s, large numbers of people turned to running; and it became an activity not limited by gender or age. As running has gained in popularity, consumer demand has expanded beyond shoes to include running gear, books, and accessories. As baby boomers age, some runners, and many others who had never exercised at all, have taken up walking, thus providing an additional market for the store. By tracking these changes and anticipating their effects, the store owners were able to continue to expand the business.

One may argue that logically any business would do this. Any store concentrating only on top-of-the-line shoes would be forced to change because of consumer demand. That may be true, but it is not the key point. If a shoe firm's managers are blind to evolving changes in their industry and maintain a strict reliance on one kind of shoe alone, other entrepreneurs will soon enter the market and fill the gap. On the other hand, if managers monitor the environment, they can anticipate these changes and modify and expand their offerings. Then the business reduces the threat of potential competition and capitalizes on an opportunity for expanding its product line and increasing its sales volume.

Demographic Changes

Demographic factors are trends in population characteristics such as age, ethnic makeup, education, family composition, and gender distribution. The U.S. Census Bureau gathers and reports these data. Changes in demographic factors can have a significant impact on an emerging business, particularly if they indicate developing trends. Changes can affect either demand for a company's products or a company's ability to hire employees.

Demand issues.   Consider the example of a local Italian restaurant that has experienced multiple shifts in its business over the past 20 years. The owners have always provided good food in a friendly atmosphere, with a fairly broad and diverse menu of Italian food. The business is noted for personalized service by friendly waiters and waitresses. Most important, the owners stress "home cooking." When an order is placed, the cooks (who are also the owners) prepare each entree with that "special touch." The business, which has existed on the same corner for more than 20 years, prospered for a number of years but then found itself facing a tough market. However, after a rocky period when survival was questionable, business is again brisk and the future looks promising.

Although many factors may help explain the performance of the restaurant through the years, demographic factors should be considered. During the 1970s and 1980s, the United States experienced a critical shift in the dining-out experience, much of it a result of the demographic shift in changing family structures. First, there were more two-career families, which explained the desire for eating out. But the attitude toward, and function of, dining out had also changed. Time was critical, and families seemed to want to eat more quickly. They desired less of a "dining experience" than a functional activity. Quickly filled orders were seen as reasonable trade-offs for limited menus with few or no frills. The Italian restaurant did not respond to these needs and therefore lost ground to more "in-touch" competitors.

Today, however, maturing baby boomers are increasingly looking for upscale, casual dining. Restaurants with quality menus are reaping the benefits as many consumers reject fast food. In particular, specialty niches, such as Italian food, appear quite popular. The restaurant described here is capitalizing on this popularity, as its specialties are again consistent with consumer desires.

Another example is the spectacular growth of services aimed at the needs of working women. Currently, the majority of married women are working. At the same time, there is tremendous growth in single-parent households. These changes provide new opportunities for creative businesses. As work-family conflicts have surfaced and moved to the social forefront, approaches for addressing and reducing those conflicts are begging for attention. In many cases, well-attuned small business owners are etching out new competitive niches. For example, KangaKab is a shuttle service that transports preschoolers to and from day care centers, filling in for parents whose hectic schedules prohibit the more traditional mom or dad shuttle.[1]

One more example illustrates how demand for products or services changes as demographics change. With the U.S. population aging, many opportunities are arising for entrepreneurs and emerging businesses. The demand for assisted-living facilities, for instance, is projected to grow at a rate of 30,000 beds a year. Senior citizens today are living far longer than earlier generations did; in fact, the single fastest growing age group is people over 100 years old! While large public companies will undoubtedly attempt to meet part of this demand, new and emerging businesses will have ample opportunity to carve out special niches and succeed. Some observers are suggesting that small businesses that operate hotel-like housing for older people will prosper. Other businesses may focus on seniors with special needs, ranging from those who simply need help with household chores and shopping to those with Alzheimer's disease.[2]

Labor issues.   While demographics affect the demand for products and services, they also affect the ability of companies to hire qualified workers. For example, one source of opportunity for teenage workers has always been the fast-food industry. This industry, often noted for less than desirable working conditions, has traditionally hired many teenagers who could not find work elsewhere. Today, however, virtually every fast-food restaurant in the country has Now Hiring signs in the window or on the marquee. Why? It's simply because fewer teenagers are available. This, coupled with a booming economy in the late 1990s, provides better opportunities for teenagers looking for work. Thus, fast-food restaurants have had to turn to an interesting but growing workforce—senior citizens.

During the 1990s, many businesses turned to temporary workers to cut the cost of full-time employees and give themselves flexibility in staffing. As the unemployment rate continues to fall, however, the pool of temporary workers nationwide is shrinking. The low supply of temporary workers is stifling the growth of some emerging businesses, particularly in the communications and software areas. Some observers even note that the crunch among temporaries may be part of a national staffing crisis.[3]

Clearly, the availability of skilled workers affects the emerging business. In fact, growth plans may have to be tempered if needed talent can't be found. Further, as the demand for labor increases and the supply of labor decreases, wages are often bid up. This, too, can significantly affect the growth actions of the emerging business. As you can see, the labor issue, which may become more threatening in the next decade or so as baby boomers begin to reach retirement age, can have pervasive effects.

Economic Changes

Economic projections or forecasts are important because of the lag time between economic changes and their effect on business forces and consumer decisions. Generally, macroeconomic information (at the national or state level) is readily available, although these data may be of little real value to emerging businesses dealing in unique and more isolated markets. Awareness of economic factors within the relevant target market therefore becomes critical. For example, business managers are concerned about factors such as movements or trends in local interest rates, unemployment levels, total sales within the community, tax rates, and availability of capital. Of course, the influence of these factors will vary considerably across firms and industries. If an emerging business is involved in consumer goods, changes in the level of disposable income also becomes an important concern.

Global Changes

Global changes offer tremendous opportunities and potential threats for emerging businesses. Numerous emerging and high-growth businesses have realized significant benefits by either selling their products or services in foreign countries or importing raw materials in order to offer their products or services in a cost-effective manner. The importance of assessing global markets has become increasingly important as a result of the development of satellite communication, cheaper and faster modes of transportation, the privatization of several overseas regions, and the emergence of economic alliances among countries.

The passage of the North American Free Trade Agreement (NAFTA) provides a significant opportunity for those U.S.-based emerging companies that can take advantage of more favorable export/import conditions with Canada and Mexico. Even before its passage, many emerging companies were keenly aware of the provisions of NAFTA and recognized its potential effects. In many cases, managers of these companies were planning the development and restructuring of their firms to avail themselves of the trade opportunities that NAFTA offered.

While foreign markets may provide many opportunities for emerging businesses, they may also expose firms to new risks. One potential risk is loss of domestic market share as a result of the emergence of foreign competition. Examples of U.S. industries that have suffered from foreign competition include automobiles, steel, and personal computers. Other detriments associated with global factors include the basic risks of doing business across national boundaries, such as fluctuations in currency exchange rates, political risk, and cultural differences.

THE CONSULTANT'S VIEWPOINT

We often hear of "lucky" companies or businesses. At some point, all businesses will experience luck—some good and some bad. A consultant should be cognizant that while some "successful" businesses may occasionally experience blind luck, so-called lucky firms are actually benefiting from a conscious effort by their managers to understand their external environment. There is little luck in business success—success usually occurs when preparedness meets opportunity, not through luck.

External Focus

Strategic planning is an externally driven process. Monitoring the external environment signals what a firm does well and where it needs to improve. Rather than first analyzing a firm and then analyzing its environment, an effective consultant will initially understand the firm's external environment. Understanding general environmental factors helps in forecasting future industry trends and directions along with helping to assess opportunities and threats in the industry. Understanding the environment must precede a constructive assessment of internal operations. In short, only after a complete external analysis is finished should a consultant begin to assess the firm's internal operations.

Driving Forces

Driving forces are major factors that influence the future direction of an industry. A comprehensive analysis of an industry can yield an array of factors that may lead to future industry trends. However, only the most important of these factors will become driving forces for industry change.

Two types of industry drivers exist: demand drivers and competitive drivers. Demand drivers are factors that affect future demand in the industry. For example, as we discussed earlier in this chapter, increasing health consciousness has created tremendous opportunities in health-related businesses. Health consciousness is therefore the demand driver. This same social characteristic—health consciousness—has had a substantial negative effect on demand in other industries. Consider the cigarette industry. For decades smoking was considered the norm. As a result of increasing concern with health consciousness, not only are we smoking fewer cigarettes, but most public places are now designated as nonsmoking areas, and California is a nonsmoking state. Clearly, increases in health consciousness have decreased demand in the cigarette industry.[4]

Competitive drivers, the second type of industry driver, affect how companies within an industry compete. Take, for example, the stock brokerage industry. Until deregulation of the banking industry in 1987, stockbrokers competed only against other stockbrokers. Following banking industry deregulation, banks were allowed to sell stocks, which completely changed the nature of competition in the brokerage industry. More recently, technological developments providing Internet privacy through encryption programs have allowed discount brokers to change the nature of competition in the industry again by operating on the Internet.

The ultimate goal of an effective external analysis is to identify the major underlying drivers for the industry. The key word when identifying drivers is "major." Quite often analysts will use a "shotgun approach" in an attempt to cover any possible drivers. Some drivers may be extremely important to determining the future of the industry but others may have minimal impact. A good rule of thumb is to identify no more than three demand drivers and three competitive drivers. Limiting the number of drivers forces a consultant to critically compare and contrast the relative importance of each one.

DISCUSSION QUESTIONS

1. Why is it critical for a manager to take a proactive stance in today's business world?
2. How do you determine if a current trend is an industry driver?
3. Explain briefly which general environment information is most relevant for the following:
   a. shoe repair shop
   b. car dealer
   c. liquor store
   d. computer software company
   e. manufacturer of tool and die equipment
4. Why is it important to perform an external analysis before proceeding with an internal analysis?

NOTES

1. Michael Selz, "Enterprise: From School to the Doctor's Office to Home; Ride Service Does the Driving for Parents," *The Wall Street Journal,* May 6, 1994, B1.

2. Michael Selz, "Value Based Companies Are Fetching Higher Prices," *The Wall Street Journal,* May 19, 1998, B2.

3. Linda Davidson, "The Temp Pool's Shrinking," *Workforce* (April, 1997): 72–80.

4. Lloyd Byars, Leslie Rue, and Shakar Zahra, *Strategic Management* (Chicago: Irwin, 1996).

CHAPTER 5

ENVIRONMENTAL ANALYSIS— INDUSTRY ENVIRONMENT

W hereas Chapter 4 discussed the general or macroenvironment, this chapter focuses on the industry and competitive environment. Industry and competitive factors may indicate whether an industry is growing or declining, who the major competitors are, what important supplier links exist, and issues regarding the labor force. When you finish reading this chapter, you should be able to

- explain the influence of competition on an industry;
- identify sources of external information;
- determine which information should be monitored carefully and which should be only casually assessed;
- understand methods of collecting and analyzing data; and
- recognize how to use competitive information.

Once the macroenvironment has been sufficiently examined, analysis should turn to the industry. Five factors should be addressed: the general nature of the industry, its growth rate, dynamics of the competition, characteristics of consumers, and dependence on suppliers.

NATURE OF THE INDUSTRY

Owners and managers must consider whether such things as technology, product quality, distribution channels, and product obsolescence are changing in their industry. Understanding the nature of the industry gives the manager of an emerging business a feel for how successful particular strategies may be. Is the industry constantly updating and using state-of-the-art equipment, or does it rely on existing equipment? Do customers in the industry demand high-quality products and service, or are they willing to accept whatever is produced? Is the industry in a product market or a service market? Is the industry part of the consumer market or does it sell its products to intermediary firms? Are products manufactured totally within a single company or do subcontractors make components?

Incremental versus Radical Changes

Industries generally change slowly. Incremental changes, of which numerous examples exist, are based on improvements to existing knowledge or technology. Consider the computer hardware and software industries. Intel has made several improvements to the speed of its processors, including the 8088, 286, 386, 486, Pentium, and Pentium II; and Microsoft has been successful with incremental improvements in its Windows 3.1, Windows 3.11, Windows 95, and Windows 98.

Occasionally, an industry will experience a radical change, but radical changes are rare. When they do occur, however, they usually completely replace the need for existing products. The quartz watch completely replaced windup watches. Word processors have replaced typewriters. Advances in the Internet are replacing the need for many traditional marketing mediums. Many people today don't remember the mimeograph machines that were made obsolete by photocopiers. Mom and pop grocery stores essentially no longer exist. And while an effective manager should be able to anticipate incremental industry changes, radical changes are far more difficult to predict.

INDUSTRY GROWTH RATE

A firm competing in a high-growth market has far different opportunities and constraints than one that competes in a mature or declining market. In a growth environment, errors and inefficiencies can be tolerated. In a low-growth market with limited profits, errors can be fatal.

The concept of product life cycle may be a useful analytical tool in examining an industry's growth rate. Typically, as noted in Figure 5.1, products are seen as passing through four distinct developmental stages. The stage a product is in in this continuum can critically affect the business because each stage is accompanied by a unique series of opportunities and difficulties. For example, if a company's products are in the latter stages of the cycle (late maturity or decline), significant future problems may arise. This is particularly true if attractive alternative products are being offered by competitors and the business does not possess a strong market share. Managers may need to search for new products or reposition the business to deal with this threat.

Managers must also understand how long it will take for products to move through the stages of the life cycle. Products may be approaching maturity, but if this stage is seen as lasting for a lengthy period, the impetus for immediate action is lessened. Similarly, relying too heavily on a product caught for too long in the introduction stage may adversely affect sales. Many factors, including the availability of substitutes and shifts in consumer tastes and preferences, will affect the rapidity of movement through the product stages. Failing to understand the level and extent of demand can produce harsh consequences. Identifying the current life-cycle position correctly and enacting a strategy consistent with these readings can be important factors of success.

FIGURE 5.1   STAGES IN PRODUCT LIFE CYCLE

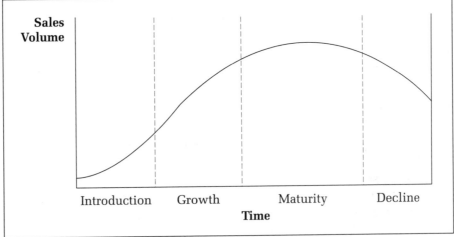

The strategic impact of shifting life-cycle stages is demonstrated in Profile 5.1. Fitness, as a social trend, certainly was a theme that captured the 1980s and fueled the growth of related industries. But the obsession with fitness reached its peak by the latter part of the 1980s and began to decline. In fact, recent statistics indicate that overall participation in exercise and strenuous activity is declining.[1] The decline seems to be across all age groups and therefore does not appear to be the result of an aging population. Americans seem to be moderating their exercise programs and focusing on relatively less strenuous activities like walking, swimming, and biking. Manufacturers in fitness and related industries must realize they are likely to experience rapid life cycles. Typically, these product areas experience accelerated growth, early maturity, and speedy declines as fickle consumers change attitudes, interests, and leisure lifestyles at a dizzying pace. Rowing machines, aerobic videos, and perhaps even jogging accessories have felt the consequences of consumer fickleness.

The nature of industry capacity must also be addressed. If demand is strong but industry capacity limited, businesses can take risks and exercise considerable flexibility. However, as industry capacity increases relative to demand, operational efficiency and cost control become critical, and weaker firms are likely to be driven out of markets.

COMPETITIVE RIVALRY[2]

One of the most critical parts of environmental analysis deals with competitive assessment. In many regards, the competition is the most visible, commonly perceived threat an emerging business faces. For example, do the firms in the industry compete only indirectly and coexist peacefully, or do they compete aggressively and attempt to drive each other from the marketplace? Is the competition price based, quality based, service based, or a combination of all three?

Included in the dynamics of the competition is the relative size and market share. Some industries may be dominated by two or three major competitors. Competing in such markets is extremely difficult for smaller companies. Other industries are highly fragmented with no dominant players. Still others may have a few national firms along with a number of small niche firms, such as the restaurant industry where national chains

PROFILE 5.1

NEW BALANCE ATHLETIC SHOE, INC.

In 1972 Jim Davis paid $100,000 to buy New Balance Athletic Shoe, Inc. This small, sleepy shoe manufacturer had been in existence for more than 60 years and had been making athletic shoes for about 10 years. Davis's purchase coincided perfectly with market demands, as the fitness and running movements were poised to explode on the American scene. As physical fitness became a national obsession during the 1980s, the athletic footwear business experienced annual growth rates as high as 20 percent. Typical of an industry with rocketing growth, new manufacturers emerged to meet the demand.

With the market soaring, Davis's strategy during the early years was quite basic—manufacture a quality product and get it into the hands of anxious buyers. New Balance, like many small businesses in this industry, pursued a follower strategy. Industry leaders Nike and Reebok dictated product movements and New Balance mirrored their actions. Unfortunately, New Balance followed the leaders as they expanded into an ever-growing range of product areas. This splintering of manufacturing focus consistently left New Balance with insufficient levels of product in its traditionally strong running shoe market. In addition, the company suffered from low brand awareness, and few advertising dollars were available to enhance that awareness. Not surprisingly, from 1986 to 1989 the company saw growth leveling off despite continued surges in the industry.

By the early 1990s the athletic footwear industry began to contract as sales dipped industrywide. Analysts posited a number of possible explanations. Perhaps the impact of the domestic economy's recession was being felt. Perhaps the market was saturated. Perhaps consumer interests and preferences were shifting. Whatever explanation was accepted, one outcome seemed apparent: An industry shakeout was likely, and survival of all existing brand name manufacturers appeared doubtful.

Clearly, New Balance's existence depended on some very careful strategic thinking. Davis's response was to build on the business's traditional strengths and focus on a few tactical approaches that could be competitive advantages—a strategy Davis called Operation Quick Strike. Operation Quick Strike contained many planks, but certain themes were central. First, New Balance created a niche in an intensively competitive industry by focusing on width sizing. While other running shoe manufacturers offered few widths, New Balance offered ranges on some shoes from AA to EEE. Although width sizing was difficult and expensive, it enabled New Balance to develop an image as a customized manufacturer. Strong production control and just-in-time retailing supported the focus on customized quality. In addition, New Balance expanded its line with great care. Reading demographic and social trends carefully, New Balance surmised that baby boomers were in the process of switching from running to exercise walking. Accordingly, a line of walking shoes became an attractive addition to the business. Operation Quick Strike strategy also focused on increased advertising aimed at carefully selected targets that were most consistent with the themes the company wished to stress. With a growing reputation for producing quality shoes that fit better than the competition's and by selectively gearing efforts toward emerging hot segments of the market, New Balance seems positioned to be one of the more successful niche players in the highly competitive athletic footwear industry.

Today, Jim Davis still owns New Balance, but the company that has emerged includes nine vice presidents covering areas such as marketing, manufacturing, finance, and global operations. Five plants are divided between Maine and Massachusetts, and in addition to sports apparel, they make shoes for eight sports in sizes from infants' size 2 to men's size 18 in widths from 2A to 4E.

Source: Jay Finegan, "Surviving in the Nike/Reebok Jungle (New Balance Athletic Shoe, Inc.)," *Inc.,* May 1993, V15 #5, pp. 98–102; and www.newbalance.com, accessed May 15, 1998.

compete along with locally owned restaurants. What is the role of franchises in the industry being considered? Independent businesses often have a difficult time competing with franchised units because of the substantial name recognition and support provided by a national firm.

Recognizing and identifying competitors is no simple task. Competitors may take new forms as markets evolve and change. Customers' needs shift and are always being met in new and unique ways. Traditional businesses may encounter new types of competition that were not even considered in the past. Clearly, a successful new or emerging business must be attuned to the changing face of competition. For example, management must consider the entry and impact of new competition in the industry. Who are these competitors? How will they affect or modify the existing structure and balance of the industry? What happens when an industry dominated by small independents must react to the entry of large national chains or franchises? In the latter situation, the independents must recognize that the entire composition of the industry has been radically affected and must make necessary adjustments.

Consider the case of Edwards Service Station, a full-service gas station started in 1970 by Curt Edwards. A superb mechanic, Curt, along with his brother and one part-time worker, transformed the single bay, neighborhood station from a fledgling start-up to a financially thriving and well-respected operation in its first decade of existence. When Curt's son Mike joined the business in 1980, full-service stations were still dominant.

Over the next decade, however, the complexion of the industry changed dramatically. The American quest for speed and specialized service began to appear in new competitive forms. Specialized muffler and brake franchises began to drain business by offering a price structure that Curt couldn't match. Similarly, specialty oil change and lube franchises offered speed, price, and convenience options that Curt was unable to duplicate. Curt largely discounted the impact of this new competition. He knew what a service station was supposed to be, and he was sure his customers would remain loyal because of the personal attention to detail that he had always provided.

But by the early 1990s Curt was fighting a losing battle. Nationally, full-service stations were in rapid decline and accounted for only about 35 percent of the total stations in the country. Mike encouraged Curt to convert to a one-stop convenience center, emphasizing convenience store items and self-service gasoline. Not surprisingly, Curt rebelled. With true professional pride, he argued that there would always be a place for the traditional service station. By the mid-1990s, Edwards Service Station was losing money, and Curt was dipping into the savings he had set aside for his retirement. In late 1996, as Edwards closed, many observers commented that its owners had been driven out of business by a new set of competitive threats.

Initially, managers should determine the number of competing firms and their market share in the trade area. Although a precise determination of market share may not be possible, collecting sales data of competing firms may provide a general understanding of relative market share. These data may be difficult to obtain, but simply looking in the Yellow Pages of a local telephone book or visiting the chamber of commerce should at least indicate the number of competitors. It is also important to assess the strengths, weaknesses, and unique competencies of competitors in addition to strategies they seem likely to use in the future. One of the best ways to assess competitors and compare their strengths and weaknesses with one's own firm is to use a competitive analysis profile, which indicates the key factors that affect the firm's success and compares competing firms' status vis-à-vis each factor. The factors chosen for consideration may vary, but the 15 factors listed in Figure 5.2 are typical. The comparison or rating need not be extensive or particularly sophisticated, but the analysis profile provides a clear snapshot of where each firm stands in terms of the 15 factors. Such awareness allows managers to recognize threats and opportunities and then act to deal with them. Consider, for example, the case of Harley's Hardware in Profile 5.2.

CHARACTERISTICS OF CUSTOMERS

Another area of analysis is the customer target market—that specific set of individuals a business chooses to attract as its primary customers. A clear recognition of the needs, concerns, and makeup of this group is critical because marketing and promotion are designed to appeal to a target market. Products and services are not ends in and of themselves. Many small business owners forget this and become so enamored with their products or services that they fail to understand or see the customer's perspective. Products or services, no matter how well conceived and developed, will only be successful if they meet some consumer need. Shifts in consumer tastes and preferences must be constantly monitored. Under-

FIGURE 5.2   COMPETITIVE ANALYSIS PROFILE

Competitive factor	Company A	Company B	Company C	Your Company
Product uniqueness				
Relative product quality				
Price				
Service				
Availability/Convenience				
Reputation/Image				
Location				
Advertising & promotion				
Policies/Effectiveness				
Product design				
Caliber of personnel				
Raw material cost				
Financial condition				
Production capabilities				
R & D position				
Variety/Selection				

standing the demographic and social makeup of the target market—specifically its distribution according to sex, age, marital status, income, occupation, and lifestyle—helps identify its needs and concerns. Shifts in target markets often offer new opportunities for a business; for example, a restaurant located in an aging neighborhood may consider modifying menu items or offering senior citizen discounts to increase business.

In addition, managers of emerging businesses must try to identify specific factors that impact consumers' purchasing decisions for their particular product or service. Is the consumer more concerned with price,

PROFILE 5.2

HARLEY'S HARDWARE

In 1975 Harley Alexander founded Harley's Hardware, a small, full-service hardware business with 15 employees in nine departments, that is known for its friendliness. Harley hired a consultant in 1995 to address the increasing number of large do-it-yourself home centers such as Lowe's and Builder's Square that were moving into the city. In exploring Harley's external situation, the consultant relied heavily on existing data sources. For example, recent secondary data from the U.S. Census Bureau, Survey of Buying Power, Standard and Poor's Industry Surveys, *Hardware Age* magazine, and the National Retail Hardware Association provided a wealth of information. Locally, each key competitor was identified, analyzed, and compared on a series of competitive factors.

Of the many competitors in Harley's trade area, six are dominant and pose the strongest threat to Harley. A detailed competitive profile for each of these competitors, with their strengths and weaknesses, is shown below. The table gives each competitor an overall performance index—a measure of how strong each is perceived to be—based on a total point index of 125. The characteristics chosen were selected because of their relevance to shoppers at hardware stores.

Scale from 1 to 5: 1 (very poor); 2 (below average); 3 (average);
4 (above average); 5 (outstanding)

Competitive Factor	Builder's Square	Lowe's	Build Rite	Pilgrim's Pride	Garrods	Kennelly
			Firm			
	General Characteristics					
Reputation	4	5	2	3	5	4
Store hours	5	5	4	4	3	3
Speed of checkout	4	3	3	4	3	3
	Merchandise Offering					
Variety/Selection	4	5	3	3	3	2
Quality of mdse	4	4	4	3	3	3

Environment						
Store layout	4	4	4	3	3	3
Displays	4	4	4	3	3	2
Merchandising	5	5	5	4	3	2
Clutter	4	4	4	4	2	2
Cleanliness	5	5	5	4	3	2
Lighting	4	4	5	2	3	4
Inside decor	5	5	3	3	2	4
Exterior	4	3	3	4	2	3
Prices						
Values	3	3	3	3	3	3
Specials	4	4	4	3	3	3
Personnel						
Friendly/Courteous	3	4	4	2	5	3
Knowledgeable	3	4	4	3	4	4
Service level	3	4	4	3	4	3
Site						
Accessibility	4	4	4	5	5	3
Parking facilities	4	4	4	5	3	2
Visibility	5	4	3	4	4	2
Shopping pull	4	5	2	4	4	3
Walk-in traffic	4	2	2	4	3	2
Advertising						
Expenditure	5	5	3	3	2	2
In-Store/P.O.P.	4	4	3	3	1	2
Overall Performance						
Index	102	103	89	86	79	69

quality, service, availability, or reputation? A good understanding of the specific factors that drive consumers' purchasing decisions will allow an emerging small business to be more responsive to consumer needs.

In some cases, successful companies have been able to differentiate their product or service so convincingly that customers are totally dependent on the business. Customers perceive that such a product or service is unique and they can only purchase it from a specific company. For example, many avid golfers are convinced that they need the Big Bertha driver, which is produced only by Callaway. This gives Callaway great flexibility in both price and delivery.

Finally, managers of emerging businesses should assess whether any barriers to entry exist—that is, factors that discourage new companies from entering an industry. Tangible entry barriers may include capital requirements, access to information and/or distribution channels, and ownership of specific assets such as plant and equipment. Intangible entry barriers may include brand name recognition, customer loyalty, and company reputation. The combined impact of these entry barriers reduces the potential threat of new firms' entry into the market.

SUPPLIERS

Because it is important for a manager to keep abreast of suppliers and the factors affecting their success, a manager must consider the firm's relationship to suppliers in light of two factors—dependency and vulnerability. Each business will differ, often considerably, in terms of these two factors. Dependency refers to the extent to which a business depends on or requires extensive raw materials or subassemblies provided by suppliers. Some businesses are fairly self-contained and self-supporting, thereby exhibiting little dependency, whereas others are almost totally dependent on their suppliers.

Vulnerability refers to the extent to which a business would be affected by breakdowns in the supply network. Typically, business vulnerability is determined by the number of competing suppliers who could provide items for the business and the track record of these suppliers. In general, the fewer sources of supply, the more vulnerable the business is to the arbitrary actions of the existing suppliers.

Sometimes dependency and vulnerability issues surface over key customers rather then key suppliers. If, for example, a business is a captive supplier of a larger firm—that is, it sells nearly all of its products or services to one customer—then the small business is extremely vulnerable when the larger firm encounters a strike or significant downturn. In most cases the larger firm survives the trauma, but the smaller, dependent firm may not.

In considering high dependency and/or vulnerability, it is critical to be aware of forces that may affect the availability of raw materials or other components as well as their price and delivery. For example, a small company that sold fine chocolates established an extensive demand for its candies through astute marketing to local businesses, restaurants, and hotels. The profitability of the firm, and indeed its survival, was threatened, however, because it had entered into an exclusive contract with a single supplier, a small, fledgling operation located nearly 500 miles from the store. Unfortunately, as the candy store's reputation grew and demand expanded, its supplier was unable to provide the needed candies. Extensive backlogs existed and customers, quite understandably, became frustrated. Before the candy store's owners were able to sever their relationship with their supplier and search out larger, more consistent sources, customer confidence had eroded to the point that the business was doomed. Again, a careful analysis of the supplier and its capacity and ability to deliver, coupled with the firm's own projections of demand, should have enabled the candy store owners to recognize this threat early enough to circumvent and overcome the disastrous implications. Again, proacting rather than reacting is the key.

PERFORMING AN ENVIRONMENTAL ANALYSIS

General factors that may impact multiple industries, identified in Chapter 4, and industry-specific factors, identified in this chapter, should be included in a firm's environmental analysis. We're now ready to look at the actual analysis.

Environmental Threats and Opportunities Profile

The Environmental Threats and Opportunities Profile (ETOP) can be an easily used and quite beneficial tool for managers. A manager looks at the firm's environment to identify significant threats and opportunities. As used here, a "threat" is any one of a range of factors that may limit, restrict, or impede the business in the pursuit of its goals. The presence of strong competition, changing public attitudes toward a firm's products, an adverse economic climate, or the bankruptcy of a key supplier are all examples of environmental factors that may pose threats for the business.

On the other hand, an "opportunity" is any factor that offers promise or potential for moving closer or more quickly toward a firm's goals. New high-growth markets, unmet or changing customer demands, the development of new products to complement existing lines, or a general upsurge in the local economy may all produce genuine opportunities for the business. More on the use of an ETOP can be found in Chapter 7.

Deciding What to Consider

Managers conducting environmental analyses must decide which factors to track. For most emerging businesses, it is totally unrealistic to believe that all the external factors that may have some influence on the firm can be constantly studied. There is neither the time nor the resources. Moreover, much environmental information is extraneous to a particular situation and therefore has negligible effects on the business. Managers must select the specific environmental factors that have the most critical impact on their firm—demand drivers and competitive drivers. These become the factors to track, study, and analyze. Although certain factors may be common to all firms, each company's managers will concentrate on a few key environmental factors peculiar to their situation. For example, all emerging businesses are affected by the economic situation of their particular community or trade area, but the need to track and monitor specific economic changes differs greatly from business to business.

A local variety store may wonder whether interest rates and unemployment are affecting its business. However, because the bulk of its sales comes from low-price, high-turnover items, interest rates and unemployment don't visibly impact the store's sales. In comparison, a growing woodworking business that specializes in the crafting and building of kitchen cabinets is in a much different situation because its sales represent investments by consumers in their homes. Kitchen cabinets are expensive, a luxury that consumers might postpone if economic times are tough. The firm's management knows that as interest rates and unemployment climb, consumers are less likely to consider purchasing new kitchen cabinets. Therefore, in developing their environmental analysis, these managers closely monitor interest rates and unemployment shifts as indicators of their projected level of business activity.

Importance of Historical Trends

One way to be sure which external factors are most important to a business, both today and in the near future, is to rely on historical trends. A careful examination of the past may reveal the environmental factors that have most critically affected the business and are relevant for future consideration. In spite of the considerable merit and value to this approach, two problems exist in using historical evidence. First, these historical data may not be available because the variables may not have been monitored carefully in the past. Second, historical evidence may not be relevant to the firm's future needs because the emerging business often exists in a rapidly changing, volatile environment.

It may be unrealistic and even dangerous to assume that past trends are indicative of future business conditions. Therefore, forward-oriented, insightful, proactive thinking may be lost if one adheres totally to historical trends. This does not imply that past records and trends don't provide meaningful and interesting input that should be considered. It does imply that the firm needs to consider more than just historical records—to extend beyond these records. To the extent that it is available and relevant, historical information is valuable, but it is the beginning rather than the end of the analysis. Historical information is valuable to identify underlying trends. The difficulty in forecasting is attempting to assess the potential impact of general and industry-specific factors on the future of an industry.

Another caveat is that organizational success may foster an attitude of invincibility and prompt managers of emerging businesses to refrain from devoting the necessary energy to environmental analysis. In fact, a firm's past success can be a formidable barrier to planning and change. An argument is often heard: "We've been doing it this way, and we've been successful. Why should we change now?" Businesses with such an outlook are forced to change when the bottom line suddenly shows declining results. This doesn't mean that the business must always be in a state of flux; indeed, managers may determine there's no need for change. But a decision not to change must be based on careful analysis and evaluation, not on complacency. If a manager continually assesses, analyzes, and interprets key environmental cues, the basis for decisions is grounded in thoughtful reason.

THE CONSULTANT'S VIEWPOINT

Environmental and competitive analysis must be ongoing. Just as a firm's environment is continually in a state of flux and evolution, the firm's analysis efforts must be similarly dynamic. When times get tough and a business is troubled, many owners of emerging businesses turn their backs on environmental analysis, arguing they are confronted by too many pressing problems to spend the time and energy necessary to deal with environmental concerns. Such reasoning is dangerous and may serve to exacerbate an already difficult situation. How can the business make the necessary decisions to reorient its business and adjust its strategic outlook without a keen awareness of its key environmental concerns? Environmental assessment and analysis form the basis for overcoming the firm's problems. Rather than being a time-consuming barrier, environmental analysis is a tool for corrective action.

Sources of External Information

A consultant may secure information necessary for environmental analysis from a number of sources. These may be secondary (existing) sources or such primary sources as market research, customer interviews, or a study of competitors' products. Sources of information can also be distinguished as internal to the firm (for example, management expertise) or external to the firm (for example, government publications). Figure 5.3 illustrates four potential sources of information based on the distinctions between primary versus secondary data and internal versus external data. Whichever approach or combination of approaches is used, constant awareness, monitoring, and openness to environmental shifts and fluctuations are critical.

Collecting Primary Internal Data

The first step for a consultant in acquiring industry-level information is to meet with the management of the emerging business. Members of management spend every day of their working lives in their specific industry. Overlooking this potentially rich source of information could be extremely detrimental to gaining a comprehensive understanding of external factors.

FIGURE 5.3 ENVIRONMENTAL DATA SOURCES

	Primary	Secondary
Internal	Working with management to draw out its expertise (e.g., environmental brainstorming)	Obtaining existing data the company may have already collected (e.g., data or files on competitors and products)
External	Collection of original information from markets (e.g., customer surveys)	Use of existing industry publications (e.g., census data, trade journals, the Internet)

To identify the key environmental concerns most relevant to a business, the consultant may want to periodically engage managers in *environmental brainstorming*—an open, freewheeling discussion that zeros in on the dynamics of a firm's particular environment. Brainstorming not only solicits important contributions from employees but is also an excellent vehicle for communication. Discussing the needs and direction of the business can foster understanding by, and commitment from, key employees.

Questions about how often brainstorming meetings should be held, who should attend, and how long they should last are difficult to answer, but we'll offer some guidelines. The timing of brainstorming sessions is dictated by the rate of change presently taking place in the industry. A business that exists in a fairly stable industry with few contemplated changes can afford to meet less often. A business in a growing or evolving industry that is inundated with new forces, demands, technology, and competition will be forced to have more frequent sessions. At a minimum, these sessions should occur annually, with more volatile industries convening perhaps every six months.

Three to four hours should be allotted for such sessions. Once the program is in place, employees can do the necessary premeeting preparation on their own time, thereby shortening the meeting time. Initially, however, it is important to allow enough time for good, creative points to surface. Participants should include all employees who have key contacts with the environment. For example, top salespeople or marketing people, financial people, those who contact or deal with customers and suppliers, and the board of directors (if there is one) would be reasonable persons to invite to share their comments.

Procedurally, the consultant can facilitate an environmental brainstorming session in a number of ways, although a fairly structured format is preferable (at least for the initial session). Asking participants to prepare an Environmental Threats and Opportunities Profile may start the session. (This approach to the ETOP is slightly modified from traditional parlance so that it is more relevant to the needs of the specific business.) First, ask participants to list (independently) the key environmental threats and opportunities that they see for the business both today and for the next year.

Reaching conclusions is not important at this stage. The object is to bring ideas and points for thought to the surface. It is probably best to accept everyone's suggestions without comment, waiting until later to reflect, analyze, and pare down the list.

Once participants have listed their threats and opportunities, they should rate each factor in terms of its impact on or significance to the firm. It probably isn't necessary to prescribe a detailed rating scheme—try asking participants to rate each factor as extremely significant, significant but not of the highest priority, or only mildly significant.

After all items have been rated, participants then present their ratings along with their justification or reasoning. Concentrate on commonalties—these will require little discussion. If everyone lists new competition as a key threat and assigns it the highest priority, then this factor clearly becomes an area of needed focus. If differences exist, participants should discuss them. For example, why does one participant recognize suppliers as being a critical threat when no one else even lists this factor? Maybe this person knows something no one else does, or perhaps he or she is off base. Nevertheless, the input and ensuing discussion are critical.

The process takes time, but it forces key personnel to become involved in the planning process and provides valuable information that may be unavailable or insufficiently detailed in historical analysis. The composite listing/rating that evolves, in conjunction with insights gained from historical data, identifies the environmental factors the firm will attempt to track, and information about these factors needs to be constantly gathered and monitored. It is important that the business realize environmental analysis is an ongoing task. Figure 5.4 provides an overview of guides to environmental brainstorming.

FIGURE 5.4   GUIDES TO ENVIRONMENTAL BRAINSTORMING

Area of Consideration	Explanation
How often to meet?	Depends largely on industry At least annually More often for rapidly changing, more dynamic industries
Who should attend?	Top salespeople Top marketing people Top finance people Those in direct contact with customers Those in direct contact with suppliers Board of directors
Preplanning?	All participants bring to the session any data relevant to their areas of expertise
Meeting dynamics?	Each participant shares information Participants prepare and rate ETOPs ETOPs and rating are shared and discussed Commonalties are noted Priorities are established

Collecting Primary External Information

Collection of primary external data consists of obtaining information directly from individuals outside the organization. It may include focus groups, interviews or surveys with suppliers, customers, and competitors. When deciding how to collect data, the consultant should first consider what types of information should be drawn from the research. For example, let's assume a company is interested in segmenting a customer market. A survey may be designed to measure how respondents rate several purchasing drivers (e.g., price, quality, serviceability, reputation, and delivery). In addition, the survey should identify demographic factors that may assist the researcher in segmenting the market (e.g., age, income level, education level, and gender). After the data are collected, the survey results may illustrate that people with a specific demographic background identify different purchasing drivers than people with a contrasting demographic background.

Collecting Secondary Internal Information

Secondary internal data are existing information the company may already have collected and put on file. Ask the company's managers for any information they may have collected about their industry and/or competitors. Even if they are not sure whether certain data would be useful, it is still necessary to review the information—the consultant should be the judge of how useful the information may be.

Collecting Secondary External Information

Secondary external information consists of existing documentation that can be found at most business libraries and on the Internet. Figure 5.5 provides a list of information sources for both macroenvironmental factors (Chapter 4) and industry-specific factors (Chapter 5).

DISCUSSION QUESTIONS

1. For a retail store, what are the best sources of information on the local economy and general conditions?
2. How can I find information about my competitors' prices, services, profits, and strategies if
   a. they are publicly held companies?
   b. they are privately held companies?
3. How does a manager use historical data when forecasting future trends?
4. What are the advantages and disadvantages of using an industry life-cycle model?

NOTES

1. John P. Robinson and Geoffrey Godbey, "Has Fitness Peaked?" *American Demographics* 15, no. 9 (September 1993): 36–42.
2. The following discussion draws on Michael E. Porter, *Competitive Strategy* (New York: Free Press, 1980).

FIGURE 5.5   <u>SOURCES OF ENVIRONMENTAL INFORMATION</u>

Factor	Sources
Technological	*Technological Forecasts* (PricewaterhouseCoopers) *Predicasts Forecasts* Industry trade associations and journals
Legal	Industry trade association reports and journals nii.nist.gov/ (accessed 6/3/98)
Social	*Statistical Abstract of the United States* *Statistical Abstract of the World* *Survey of Consumers* (University of Michigan Institute for Social Research)
Demographics	*U.S. Bureau of Census* *Demographic Yearbook of the United States* *Statistical Yearbook* Area chamber of commerce www.easidemographics.com (accessed 6/3/98) www.census.gov (accessed 6/3/98)
Economic	*Economic Indicators* *World Fact Book* *Economic Report of the President* *Standard and Poor's Industry Surveys* *Census of Manufacturing/Retail* Chamber of commerce reports www.bls.gov (accessed 6/3/98) www.fcnbd.com (accessed 6/3/98) www.census.gov (accessed 6/3/98)
Global	*Statistical Abstract of the World* *Management International* Economic Intelligence Unit (EIU) National Trade Data Bank (NTDB)
Industry Specific	*Market Share Reporter* *Standard and Poor's Industry Surveys* *Industry Norms and Key Business Ratios* *Robert Morris Associates* *Census of Manufacturers* Industry reports from business periodicals Trade association reports and journals Local chamber of commerce

INTERNAL ANALYSIS

This chapter extends the analysis phase of the strategic planning model by examining a firm's internal condition. The internal analysis offers a profile of the firm's operations and is geared toward pinpointing and assessing the key internal strengths and weaknesses of the firm. Chapters 4 and 5 examined external factors that may impact a firm's ability to compete. Managers should be aware of key environmental threats and opportunities before beginning the internal analysis.

This chapter is divided into four categories, each with a number of subareas. Once you have completed this chapter, you should be able to

- understand the complexities of an internal analysis;
- determine which areas of a business should be analyzed;
- measure strengths and weaknesses in a business based on external benchmarks; and
- create a company profile for a business.

VALUE OF INTERNAL ANALYSIS

Objective internal analysis is essential for at least two reasons. First, many managers of emerging small businesses have inaccurate perceptions of their company's internal state of affairs. Often, they rely on personal opinion or "feel" to assess their firm's internal condition, which may result in an unrealistic perspective of the company's capacity, potential, and areas of concern. Only through a careful and systematic internal analysis can a reasonable and meaningful profile be attained. In Profile 6.1, managers of MRM performed a careful assessment of the company's internal condition and were surprised by what they found. As the result of internal analysis and strategic planning, they realized a single supplier to their distributorship that accounted for 40 percent of MRM's sales cost far more than it contributed.

The second reason for doing an internal analysis is even more important. Essentially, internal analysis reveals whether a business has available the means for dealing with its environmental opportunities and threats—a critical revelation. It can change the focus of a company's activities and strategies and, in many situations, save the business from disaster. Yet for many companies and managers, it is a forgotten step in the logical planning sequence. Business managers tend to move strategically to capture opportunities without carefully considering their ability to do so successfully.

Managers must mesh their environmental awareness and insight with a corresponding understanding of internal demands. Moving aggressively in the external environment without adequate internal support will, in most cases, lead to serious difficulties. These points are reinforced quite dramatically in the now classic example of Osborne Computers, described in Profile 6.2.

ELEMENTS OF INTERNAL ANALYSIS

Internal analysis requires time and commitment. It's not unusual for companies to spend several weeks analyzing their strengths and weaknesses. The rewards for conducting the analysis, however, are many.

PROFILE 6.1

Giving Up Your Best Customer

Tony Rigato is owner and CEO of MRM, a $10 million distributor of pneumatic industrial components in Novi, Michigan. A distributor is a business that buys products in bulk from manufacturers and then sells them to a number of customers. Its customers may be retailers, industrial customers, or consumers, depending on the nature of the business. When he was first introduced to strategic planning, Rigato had no intention of dropping his key supplier. But sometimes strategic planning uncovers information that you don't really expect.

As part of MRM's strategic planning process, which was repeated annually, 12 objectives were determined. One of these was to increase sales from $4 million to $10 million in three years, which still begs the question, "If the goal is to more than double sales in three years, why would you jettison a supplier that accounts for 40 percent of your sales?" The answer came from the analysis that goes along with strategic planning. Rigato discovered, as he and his team went through a brutally honest internal analysis, that MRM was spending 70 percent of its resources getting 40 percent of its sales. Clearly, such a situation couldn't continue; alternative suppliers had to be found.

Even with some temporary setbacks as new contacts were formed, MRM's decision to drop its major supplier was necessary and correct. By 1997, MRM's sales had hit $13.5 million, profitability had increased substantially, and employee turnover reached an all-time low. Rigato noted that "none of what we've been able to accomplish would have been possible without strategic planning."

Source: Donna Fenn, "No More Business as Usual," *Inc.,* November 1997, pp. 114, 119.

PROFILE 6.2

OSBORNE COMPUTER CORPORATION

In the early 1980s, Adam Osborne revolutionized the personal computer industry. By carefully assessing consumer needs followed by astute marketing, Osborne built his empire to one that by 1983 was selling 10,000 machines a month and earning an annual revenue of more than $100 million. (Keep in mind that the personal computer industry was in its infancy in the early 1980s.)

His approach was basic: He delivered a technologically sound machine (Osborne I), sold it at two-thirds the price of its closest competitor, offered over $1,500 worth of brand name software at no additional cost, and packaged it in a portable, 26-pound easy-to-carry unit. (Laptops did not exist then!)

When the Osborne I proved successful, competitors recognized the viability of this new segment of the computer business and aggressively entered the market with their own products. To counter, Osborne developed a new portable computer, the Osborne Executive, that improved on the original Osborne I by providing more memory storage and a larger screen, yet still sold for a relatively attractive $2,495. Further, the Executive was to be IBM compatible.

Osborne began publicizing the machine in electronics journals and publications well in advance of its expected delivery date. Because of the notable improvements over the Osborne I, dealers were impressed. In fact, they were so impressed that they stopped orders of the Osborne I to wait for the arrival of the Executive.

But production delays plagued the Executive. Publicity was distributed, dealers were ready to order, but the machine was not yet available. At the same time, sales of Osborne I were falling. Osborne had so effectively convinced dealers of the power of his new machine that they abandoned the original one. Unfortunately, the Executive couldn't be delivered. A two-and-a-half-month period of dwindling sales brought on a debilitating cash squeeze and was one of the key factors that pushed Osborne Computer Corporation into bankruptcy.

Internal Strengths and Weaknesses

One of the most basic, yet insightful, approaches to internal analysis focuses on the identification of internal strengths and weaknesses. As the term is used here, a strength is any resource or occurrence that *helps* the business realize its objectives and strategies, capitalize on its opportunities, or defend against its threats. Conversely, a weakness is any factor that *hinders* the business from realizing its objectives and strategies, capitalizing on its opportunities, or defending against its threats.

Internal strengths and weaknesses can be divided into four categories: financial resources, marketing resources, operational resources (organizational and technical), and human resources. The relevant subcomponents are included in the internal analysis profile in Figure 6.1.

Rating Internal Strengths and Weaknesses

In developing a meaningful internal analysis or profile, some sort of evaluation or rating scheme must be used to identify strengths and weaknesses. Such a scheme should be easy to use yet comprehensive and complete. The internal analysis profile in Figure 6.1 fulfills these objectives. Each internal factor or resource examined is given one of five ratings: strong weakness, slight weakness, neutral, slight strength, or strong strength. Clearly, degrees of strength and weakness exist. A given factor or resource must be assessed and weighted as being slight, neutral, or strong. Further, some factors may not be currently relevant but may still be included in the analysis if they are expected to become relevant in the near future.

Evidence such as financial ratios, defective-product rates, or labor turnover data may provide an objective basis for choosing a particular rating category, but such evidence is often unavailable. Managers, for example, may want to know the effectiveness of advertising but have no figures relating sales to advertising efforts, so they use judgmental approaches. Of course, steps addressed in the following section can be taken to build confidence and objectivity into these judgments.

Many variables are available for analysis. Within the financial area alone, over two dozen ratios could be considered. Many of these, however, may not be relevant for some businesses and may be unavailable for others. Variables should be selected that meet three requirements. First, they must be relevant. Second, they must be assessed with at least a reasonable degree of accuracy. Third, they must be within the owner's range

FIGURE 6.1   INTERNAL ANALYSIS PROFILE

Internal Resource	Strong Weakness	Slight Weakness	Neutral	Slight Strength	Strong Strength
FINANCIAL RESOURCES					
Overall performance					
Ability to raise capital					
Cash position					
MARKETING RESOURCES					
Market performance					
Knowledge of markets					
Location					
Product					
Advertising and promotion					
Price					
Image					
Distribution					
OPERATIONAL RESOURCES					
Production facilities					
Access to suppliers					
Inventory control					
Quality control					
Organizational structure					
HUMAN RESOURCES					
Number of employees					
Top management abilities					
Relevancy of skills					
Morale					
Compensation					

of influence. Only if the variables meet all three tests are they useful for analyzing and improving the firm's condition.

As shown in Figure 6.1, the variables chosen here (and discussed in sections that follow) are in the categories of financial condition, marketing capabilities, operational efficiency, and human resources. Keep in mind that the categories chosen and the variables analyzed may differ depending on the type of company and industry involved.

FINANCIAL RESOURCE ANALYSIS

In a new business, adequate financial resources often mean the difference between success and failure. In an existing but emerging firm, financial resources are a key part of its growth strategy. For example, excellent environmental opportunities may be identified along with reasonable strategies for capitalizing on them. But without adequate financial resources, the strategies may lay dormant for years, never to be implemented. Even more disturbing, a business may be forced to halt a viable project or program in midstream after its financial capacity has been exhausted. Analyzing financial resources can help identify such problems and prevent such disappointing occurrences.

Problems uncovered in the financial analysis may catch the manager's attention. The problems may be in marketing, inventory control, purchasing, pricing, or perhaps even human resources. But the problems eventually show up in financial performance, and the financial analysis therefore becomes the most obvious starting point.

As an owner or manager begins to examine and rate the relative strength of the firm's financial resources, certain caveats must be kept in mind. Existing financial statements should be used as *tools* in the evaluation process; they rely on historical data and thus are pictures of past behavior. It is reasonable to assume that past behavior can indicate present capacity and future expectations. Yet, particularly for emerging small businesses, these figures may not capture the firm's vitality or future prospects.

Rapid growth in an industry dictates that firms continuously invest capital to keep up with the demand for their products, which means that emerging businesses will often be in a weak financial condition. Their financial condition may appear on paper to be far more questionable than a similar business that is not encountering growth. For example, many growth-oriented businesses go public without ever having made a profit. But their potential for growth is so great that investors are willing to infuse their cash into the business.

In addition, financial analysis is only as powerful as the extent and quality of the information on which it is based. If a firm's managers have gathered little meaningful data or have prepared scant and limited statements, it becomes much more difficult to draw worthwhile financial conclusions. It is imperative therefore that managers do their homework and create financial reports that provide accurate information.

Many managers find it useful to compare their financial picture against some general standard. Understandably, they want to know how they stack up against their industry's performance norms. Such comparisons can be useful barometers or checkpoints for the business but must be approached with some degree of caution. Financial ratios, for example, may be significantly higher or lower than comparative standards yet have a perfectly plausible explanation. Therefore, comparisons are only one way to assess the company's financial condition.

Comparative financial information may come from a variety of sources. Dun and Bradstreet publishes *Industry Norms and Key Business Ratios;* Robert Morris Associates publishes *Annual Statement Studies;* and Leo Troy publishes the *Almanac of Business and Industrial Financial Ratios.* Each covers a vast number of industries, typically further broken down by company asset size and sales. The Robert Morris Associates volume seems especially useful for new and emerging companies. Additional comparative information may be obtained from trade associations, trade magazines, annual reports of publicly held competitors, and other sources specifically related to particular industries.

Comparative Financial Summaries

The balance sheet and income statement are important first steps in analyzing the financial health of a company. They are especially useful when presented both in dollars and in percentages and compared over a period of several years. Although changes are never easy to assess, the comparative statements can be quite useful when studied specifically to determine the causes of change.

Consider the balance sheet (Figure 6.2) and income statement (Figure 6.3) for Waverly Custom Jewelers, a small corporation that has been in business for several years. Recently, with the rise in disposable income, Waverly has experienced a surge of growth. Its statements show Waverly's financial summaries for each of the past four years. This historical view can offer some interesting insights regarding key changes or trends; for example, there has been considerable growth in total assets for the firm over the four years.

FIGURE 6.2   <u>WAVERLY CUSTOM JEWELERS COMPARATIVE BALANCE SHEETS</u>

	1995	1996	1997	1998
Current assets				
Cash	$ 11,100	$ 13,500	$ 20,500	$ 20,200
Accounts receivable	13,500	16,900	24,700	27,500
Inventory	110,400	147,900	157,000	165,800
Prepaid expenses	9,000	8,000	7,000	8,000
TOTAL CURRENT ASSETS	$144,000	$186,300	$209,200	$221,500
Fixed assets				
Equipment	46,400	46,400	76,400	96,400
Less depreciation	(11,600)	(23,200)	(37,800)	(57,400)
TOTAL ASSETS	$178,800	$209,500	$247,800	$260,500
Current liabilities				
Accounts payable	$ 21,600	$ 31,000	$ 19,000	$ 20,000
Expenses payable	16,200	18,800	14,400	15,000
Interest payable	900	1,000	1,600	1,000
Tax payable	3,000	2,000	12,000	3,000
Note payable	52,000	32,000	20,000	10,000
TOTAL CURRENT LIABILITIES	$ 93,700	$ 84,800	$ 67,000	$ 49,000
Long-term liabilities				
Long-term loan	0	27,000	47,000	40,000
TOTAL LIABILITIES	$ 93,700	$111,800	$114,000	$ 89,000
Owner's equity				
Stock	$ 70,100	$ 70,100	$ 70,100	$ 70,100
Retained earnings	15,000	27,600	63,700	101,400
TOTAL LIABILITIES & OWNER'S EQUITY	$178,800	$209,500	$247,800	$260,500

FIGURE 6.3 WAVERLY CUSTOM JEWELERS COMPARATIVE INCOME STATEMENTS

	1995	1996	1997	1998
Net sales	$421,200	$489,000	$464,000	$493,000
Cost of goods sold	280,800	342,300	278,400	295,200
Gross profit on sales	$140,400	$146,700	$185,600	$197,800
Expenses				
Operating expenses	93,600	104,000	92,100	97,800
Depreciation expense	11,600	11,600	14,600	19,600
Net income from operations	$ 35,200	$ 31,100	$ 78,900	$ 80,400
Less interest expense	5,200	5,900	6,700	5,000
Net income before tax	$ 30,000	$ 25,200	$ 72,200	$ 75,400
Less income tax expense	15,000	12,600	36,100	37,700
NET INCOME	$ 15,000	$ 12,600	$ 36,100	$ 37,700

Looking at the year-to-year changes in each category, we see that cash grew slowly in 1996, substantially in 1997, and remained almost constant in 1998. As shown in Figure 6.3, sales increased, decreased, and then increased again. Net income fell when sales increased, rose when sales decreased, and then increased as sales went to the high level of 1998. This information gives Waverly's managers hints as to problems that may need further study.

Identifying the causes of the reported changes can be quite difficult. Generally, managers or consultants must know the business and the various conditions and occurrences that could account for the pattern of changes in order to offer reasonable explanations and evaluations.

Comparative Percentage Summaries

It's often useful to present the items on the balance sheet as percentages of total assets (see Figure 6.4); similarly, income statement items can be presented as percentages of total sales (see Figure 6.5). These procedures provide a clearer basis for year-to-year comparisons and enable fluctuations and deviations to be readily noticed. Operating results (Figure 6.5) suffered in 1996, as compared to 1995, when cost of goods sold

FIGURE 6.4 COMPARATIVE BALANCE SHEET PERCENTAGES (VERTICAL ANALYSIS)

	Industry Average	1995 %	1996 %	1997 %	1998 %
Current assets					
Cash	6	6	7	8	8
Accounts receivable (net)	9	7	8	10	11
Inventory	66	62	70	64	63
Prepaid expenses	n/a	5	4	3	3
Total current assets	85	80	89	85	85
Long-term assets					
Equipment, furniture & fixtures	10	20	11	15	15
TOTAL ASSETS	100**	100	100	100	100
Current liabilities					
Merchandise payable	18	12	15	8	8
Operating expenses payable	n/a	9	9	6	6
Interest payable	n/a	1	1	1	1
Income tax payable	n/a	2	1	5	1
Short-term notes payable	13	29	15	8	4
Total current liabilities	40**	53	41	28	20
Long-term liabilities					
Notes payable	14	0	13	19	15
Owner's equity					
Common stock	41	39	33	28	26
Retained earnings*		8	13	25	39
TOTAL LIABILITIES & OWNER'S EQUITY	100**	100	100	100	100

* Stock and retained earnings combined = 41 percent
** Totals do not match individual items because of differences in reporting.
n/a = not reported in Robert Morris Associates

increased as a percentage of sales revenue. The picture changed in 1997 when Waverly was able to raise its prices considerably with a much lower decrease in sales, giving a much better gross profit percentage that year. With the lower level of activity, operating expenses decreased as a percentage of sales revenue. Growth in sales in 1998 led to a small increase in after-tax net income over 1997 with almost no changes in percentages.

FIGURE 6.5   COMPARATIVE INCOME STATEMENT PERCENTAGES (VERTICAL ANALYSIS)

	Industry Average	1995 %	1996 %	1997 %	1998 %
Net sales	100	100	100	100	100
Cost of goods sold	54	67	70	60	60
Gross profit on sales	46	33	30	40	40
Expenses:					
Operating expenses	40	22	22	20	20
Depreciation expense	n/a	3	2	3	4
Net income from operations	5.2	8	6	17	16
Less interest expense	n/a	1	1	1	1
Net income before tax	3.7	7	5	16	15
Less income tax expense	n/a	3.5	2.5	8	7.5
NET INCOME	n/a	3.5	2.5	8	7.5

Figures 6.2 and 6.4 indicate that the firm became less dependent on short-term borrowed funds from 1995 to 1998. Long-term debt, which was used partially to increase inventory and partially to decrease short-term debt, was added in 1996 and 1997.

Cash Flow Statement

Despite the importance of the income statement as a financial analysis tool, the success of growing businesses may hinge more on cash flow than on net income—cash is the lifeblood of a business. A business may show a profit on paper and still not have sufficient cash to operate for at least three reasons.

First, if sales are made on credit, the registering of a sale does not mean that cash is received. The firm may not receive the actual cash for 60 to 90 days. Second, payments for inventory may be required at the time of ordering or receiving products, but the actual products may not be sold for several months. Third, some expenses may be recorded on a uniform monthly basis when payment for the expense is either quarterly or annually. Cash outflows therefore seldom match cash inflows, and a business can be cash poor in spite of making money on every sale, as illustrated using the Waverly Custom Jewelers case.

Figure 6.6 shows Waverly's cash flow for each month of 1998. Total sales for the year are the same as in Figure 6.3, but Waverly's sales fluctu-

FIGURE 6.6 WAVERLY CUSTOM JEWELERS CASH FLOW STATEMENT 1998

	Jan	Feb	Mar	Apr	May	Jun	Jul	Aug	Sep	Oct	Nov	Dec	TOTAL
Cash inflows													
Cash sales	$ 9,500	$28,500	$ 9,700	$ 10,500	$25,200	$10,200	$ 7,500	$ 6,800	$ 7,800	$ 7,550	$ 50,500	$ 72,750	$246,500
A/R receipts	71,250	9,500	28,500	9,700	10,500	25,200	10,200	7,500	6,800	7,800	7,550	50,500	245,000
Cash outflows													
Inventory	34,200	11,640	12,600	30,240	12,240	9,000	8,160	9,360	9,060	60,600	87,300	10,200	294,600
Rent	2,000	2,000	2,000	2,000	2,000	2,000	2,000	2,000	2,000	2,000	2,000	2,000	24,000
Advertising					500	1,000				500	2,000	2,000	6,000
Salaries	2,000	2,000	2,000	2,000	2,000	2,000	2,000	2,000	2,000	2,000	2,000	2,000	24,000
Wages	2,775	2,775	2,775	2,775	2,775	2,775	2,775	2,775	2,775	2,775	4,000	4,000	35,750
Loan payments	750	750	750	750	750	750	750	750	750	750	750	750	9,000
Taxes		9,425			9,425			9,425			9,425		37,700
Miscellaneous	1,200	975	825	1,100	400	800	1,050	875	900	1,100	850	1,100	11,275
NET CASH FLOW	$37,825	$ 8,435	$17,250	$-18,665	$ 5,610	$17,075	$ 965	$-12,885	$-2,885	$-54,375	$-50,275	$101,200	$ 49,175

ate by season. A high percentage of sales occurs in November and December, when customers purchase Christmas presents. Another relatively high peak is in May and June because of graduations, weddings, Mother's Day, and Father's Day. A brief surge in sales comes in February just before Valentine's Day. Sales are also not always in cash: some are on credit cards and some on store credit. Assume for this example that half the sales are cash and the remainder are paid in the following month. Note that jewelry is purchased by the store two months before it is sold. Waverly has a good credit rating and makes its purchases on credit, typically making payment the month after purchases. Thus, for Waverly, cash payments precede sales by one month. Miscellaneous operating expenses are not broken down into specific expenses, but items such as insurance, attorney fees, and utilities vary over the year. Although both the inflow and the outflow of cash vary over the year, they do not vary in concert.

The importance of analyzing cash flow can be seen by even a cursory look at Waverly's financial statements. The income statement in Figure 6.3 shows total income for 1998 of $37,700. The cash flow statement in Figure 6.6 shows a net cash flow for the year of $49,175, or approximately $11,000 higher than net income. However, monthly net cash flows varied from a +$101,200 in December to a –$54,375 in October primarily because Waverly's owners were purchasing inventory in October that was sold in November and December. If a business similar to Waverly Custom Jewelers was low in cash and then experienced a month like October or November, it would have severe cash flow problems.

Financial Ratios

Analyzing the three financial statements—balance sheet, income statement, and cash flow statement—provides a wealth of information with which to assess the financial health of a business. Even more information can be obtained by tracking ratios of variables taken from the financial statements. The dozens of ratios that can be computed fall into four categories: liquidity ratios, activity ratios, leverage ratios, and profitability ratios. A few ratios from within the four categories that can be tracked and computed easily can be selected as shown in Figure 6.7.

Liquidity ratios.　These ratios indicate the firm's capacity for meeting its short-run or near-term cash obligations. In other words, these ratios help in determining whether the business has enough working capital to

FIGURE 6.7   SELECTED FINANCIAL RATIOS FOR WAVERLY JEWELERS

Comparative Current Ratios

Current Ratio = Current Assets / Current Liabilities
1995   144,000 / 93,700 = 1.5
1996   186,300 / 84,800 = 2.2   Industry average = 1.8
1997   209,200 / 67,000 = 3.1
1998   221,500 / 49,000 = 4.5

Comparative Quick Ratios

1995   33,600 / 93,700 = .36
1996   38,400 / 84,800 = .45   Industry average = .30
1997   52,200 / 67,000 = .78
1998   55,700 / 49,000 = 1.14

Comparative Inventory Turnover Ratios

1995   280,800 / (110,400 + 98,600)/2* = 2.69
1996   342,300 / (147,900 + 110,400)/2 = 2.65   Industry average = 1.2
1997   278,400 / (157,000 + 147,900)/2 = 1.83
1998   295,200 / (165,800 + 157,000)/2 = 1.83

*Beginning inventory plus ending inventory divided by 2.

Comparative Asset Turnover Ratios

1995   421,200 / 178,800 = 2.35
1996   489,000 / 209,500 = 2.33   Industry average = 1.5
1997   464,000 / 247,800 = 1.87
1998   493,000 / 260,500 = 1.89

Comparative Accounts Receivable
Turnover Ratios

1995   210,600 / (13,500 + 11,500)/2* = 16.8
1996   244,500 / (16,900 + 13,500)/2 = 16.1   Industry average = 32.5
1997   232,000 / (24,700 + 16,900)/2 = 11.2
1998   246,500 / (27,500 + 24,700)/2 = 9.4

*Beginning accounts receivable plus ending accounts receivable divided by 2.

Comparative Average Collection Period
(in days)

1995   365 / 16.8 = 21.7
1996   365 / 16.1 = 22.7   Industry average = 11.2
1997   365 / 11.2 = 32.6
1998   365 / 9.4 = 38.8

Comparative Debt-to-Assets Ratios

1995	93,700 / 178,800 = 52%
1996	111,800 / 209,500 = 53% (Industry average not available)
1997	114,000 / 247,800 = 46%
1998	89,000 / 260,500 = 34%

Comparative Debt-to-Equity Ratios

1995	93,700 / 85,100 = 110%
1996	111,800 / 97,700 = 114% Industry average = 150%
1997	114,000 / 133,800 = 85%
1998	89,000 / 171,500 = 52%

Comparative Return on Total Assets Ratios

1995	35,200 / (178,800 + 158,200)/2* = 20.9%
1996	31,100 / (209,500 + 178,800)/2 = 16% (Industry average
1997	78,900 / (247,800 + 209,500)/2 = 34.5% not available)
1998	80,400 / (260,500 + 247,800)/2 = 30.2%

*Average total assets = beginning assets plus ending assets divided by 2.

get by, pay its bills, invest in the future, take advantage of immediate opportunities, and fight off unforeseen short-term crises. The two most important of these are the current ratio and the acid test or quick ratio.

The *current ratio* is derived by dividing current assets by current liabilities. A generally accepted view is that the current ratio should be 2 to 1, but this is only a rough rule of thumb that varies considerably from industry to industry. For example, if the industry is one in which the bulk of sales are made on credit, a larger current ratio may be needed for comfort. A business like Waverly, which has a high amount of expensive inventory, would be expected to have high current assets. The size of the current ratio is a function of how the inventory is financed. If short-term debt is used, the ratio will be lower than if long-term debt or equity is used. The desirability of a high ratio also depends on how conservative management is. A very conservative manager may want high inventories, high amounts of cash, and high accounts receivable to feel secure. However, inventory uses up cash that could be used for other purposes, and a liberal accounts receivable policy means underwriting customers' debt at no interest. Further, keeping excess cash or short-term investments on hand means that those funds are not being invested to their maximum potential.

How a firm compares with its industry and how it compares with itself in previous periods are important to know. In the Waverly example, note the changes that have occurred in current ratio over the years. At the end of 1995, the ratio was below the rough rule of thumb of 2 to 1. It improved in 1996 largely because long-term debt was substituted for short-term payables. By 1998, the ratio was very strong. In fact, the current ratio suggests that the firm should now consider a better use of cash, particularly significant given that the industry average for jewelry companies of this size is only 1.8.

The *quick ratio* (sometimes called the acid test ratio) is computed by subtracting inventory from current assets and dividing the result by current liabilities. Because inventories may not be easily converted to cash, the quick ratio gives a more accurate picture of a firm's capacity for short-run response to opportunities and crises by subtracting the value of these inventories. Although considerable variability is possible, a quick ratio of 1 to 1 is typically sought; the retail jewelry industry has an extremely low quick ratio because of the value of inventory. Figure 6.7 shows the quick ratios for Waverly Custom Jewelers, which exceed the industry in each of the past four years and is quite high in 1998.

Activity ratios. These ratios offer insight into how efficiently the firm is using its resources. The *inventory turnover ratio* is computed by dividing cost of goods sold by average inventory. Again, rules of thumb vary depending on the industry. Therefore, it's valuable to compare the inventory turnover ratio in a business with the industry average as well as with a company's historical ratios. The inventory turnover ratio for Waverly has consistently exceeded the industry average, but the ratios in 1997 and 1998 were lower even though profits were higher. Waverly may have purchased more inventory than it needed when it changed its pricing strategy in 1997, and the store's inventory management probably requires additional study.

The *asset turnover ratio* is computed by dividing sales by total assets. The asset turnover ratios for Waverly Custom Jewelers show a drop in 1997 that correlates with the drop in the inventory turnover ratio, suggesting the need to study asset management.

The *accounts receivable turnover ratio* is computed by dividing annual credit sales by average accounts receivable. Accounts receivable turnover is the time it takes to collect credit sales. The ratio should be monitored carefully and compared with industry standards; it is most frequently used to check the receivables collection rate. Approximately half of Waverly's sales are on credit.

The average collection period indicates the average length of time a business must wait to collect its credit sales and is calculated by dividing 365 by the accounts receivable turnover ratio. This variable is important in cash flow analysis and is especially important when you also consider the average inventory holding period (365 days divided by the inventory turnover ratio). If an owner pays cash for inventory purchases, then that cash is not returned until the inventory turnover period plus the average collection period has passed. For example, if inventory is held an average of 35 days and the average collection period is another 25 days, the owner is waiting a total of 60 days for the return of the cash. If this figure is greater than industry norms or is increasing over time, it may mean that the business is either too liberal with its credit policy or has unusual difficulty in collections.

The average collection period over the past few years needs to be determined. Significant shifts should be examined to determine if they are caused by deliberate changes in company policies, changing customer behavior, or simply weakness in collections. The collection period for Waverly Custom Jewelers has lengthened considerably, which may be a danger signal even though the store's liquidity ratios are high.

Leverage ratios.   Leverage ratios indicate the extent to which the business's capital is secured through debt rather than equity. These figures are quite critical for the new or growing firm because its ability to raise additional capital may be affected by the present leverage position. The *debt-to-assets* ratio indicates the percentage of assets that are funded through debt and is measured by dividing total liabilities by total assets. A ratio that is too high may be risky. Too much debt may restrict growth and the ability to raise additional funds externally. Conversely, a low debt-to-assets ratio may indicate inefficient use of invested capital. Waverly shows a healthy decrease in its debt-to-assets ratio, so it may be in a position to pay out cash or to enlarge its investment in noncurrent assets.

The *debt-to-equity ratio* indicates the extent to which operating funds have been generated by the owner and is computed by dividing total debt by total owner's equity. The debt-to-equity ratio for Waverly Custom Jewelers in Figure 6.5 shows a significant decrease in reliance on debt.

An important leverage consideration for many emerging small businesses is where to obtain financing when the company's leverage position is strong. Questions of where and how the business will secure the funds necessary for its operations are often perplexing, and the answers may spell the difference between success and failure. Rare is the manager who possesses sufficient financial resources to personally fund the range of needs the business will encounter. Therefore, outside sources must be used and two fundamental concerns addressed.

First, sources of capital available to the business should be identified. The sources may be fairly informal contacts, such as loans from friends or family; or they may be more formally established institutional bases, such as commercial banks, the Small Business Administration, or suppliers' credit. Emerging businesses may also use angels—individual investors willing to invest in a few high-risk businesses—and venture capitalists. Some additional sources that may be considered include sale of stock, personal savings, and credit cards.

Recognizing sources of capital is only the first step. It is also necessary to identify and clearly understand the cost of capital. The managers of an emerging small business have to decide whether the financial cost of securing the capital is worth the gains that will accrue from applying it. Cost of capital is not limited to purely financial terms. Some capital sources impose definite restrictions on the business, affect the business's flexibility, and alter the managers' degree of control, costs that must be understood and balanced.

Profitability ratios. Profitability ratios measure a firm's financial performance and financial returns. They are important on their own as they pertain to a particular company and as they compare with industry averages. Significant deviations from industry standards or strong negative movements internally may signal that the economic viability of the business is in serious question. In short, profitability ratios give a quick, bottom-line picture of the firm's current financial results.

Gross profit margin indicates how selling activity provides the margin to cover operating costs and leave a profit balance, a ratio also reported directly on the comparative percentage statements in Figure 6.5.

The *return on total assets ratio* measures the firm's operating performance and is calculated by dividing net income from operations by average total assets. In other words, it is the rate of return on the total investment made by creditors and owners. Waverly Custom Jewelers, as should be expected, shows improvement in 1997 and 1998 as compared with 1995 and 1996. Although total assets have grown, net income has increased at a faster rate. Additional funds from incurring long-term debt seemed to do much to improve ratios and performance for this company.

Drawing Strategic Conclusions

As noted frequently above, conclusions are more difficult to draw than financial ratios are to compute. Indeed, in assessing a firm's financial state, ratios and statement comparisons must be used as tools to guide planners in their decisions.

But these measures are only one of the possible information sources that should be considered. The owner's knowledge and awareness of the business may be necessary either to temper or to augment what the financial information projects. Good sense and perspective must be used in conjunction with objective figures and computations.

Strategic thinking should pervade the entire financial analysis. For example, a low current ratio suggests that the firm could have trouble paying its bills. However, the strategic significance is that any substantial change in the net use of funds may cause the firm's liquidity position to worsen. Long-term capital may need to be secured to underwrite the strategy and clean up the current liquidity problem.

Similarly, leverage ratios may suggest strong or weak positions in regard to debt versus capital, but they may also dictate a financial strategy before a planned expansion. Interpretations of ratio analyses and financial statement information are the basis for three financial resource evaluations. First, what is the overall financial performance of the business? A number of items may need to be considered in reaching this conclusion. Next, is the firm able to raise needed capital? Cash flows, availability of internal funds, and a firm's debt position may all be important considerations. Finally, what is a firm's cash flow position?

It may appear overly simplistic to reduce the evaluation of financial resources to these three questions, but they are typically the three most critical the business owner must ask before committing to the pursuit of any objective, strategy, or environmental opportunity.

EVALUATING MARKETING RESOURCES

Marketing resources are rarely subjected to close analysis or scrutiny. A business often has no valid measure of the relative effectiveness of its marketing efforts. And because managers often fail to understand the capacity and limitations of the existing marketing system, it's necessary to evaluate the marketing function very carefully.

In analyzing the internal strengths and weaknesses of the marketing system, managers should consider eight general categories of marketing resources: market performance, knowledge of markets, location, product, advertising and promotion, price, image, and distribution.

Market Performance

A logical starting point is to evaluate or rate actual market performance. The most reasonable and tangible factor to consider is a firm's relative market share. We may occasionally have enough information about the industry, market area, and competitors to calculate an objective and accurate statement of market share. More often, only an estimate of market share can be developed based on sketchy or piecemeal data. This is especially true in new businesses whose entrepreneurs do not have a good sense of the market and in small neighborhood companies in which determining sales of other small competitors is extremely difficult.

For example, managers of Harley's Hardware Store in Chapter 5 knew that they faced competition from six other stores in their basic market area. Furthermore, they knew that three of the other stores commanded the bulk of the business. Even without any specific data, these business managers clearly understood that their firm's market share rating was relatively weak. Usually, some objective information will be available that, when complemented by sound subjective judgments, provides a pretty accurate picture of relative market share. In other words, some objective data as well as some subjective information may be available. The subjective information is not easily analyzed, but experienced managers can make inferences from it.

Market share is a rather limited indicator of a company's performance that addresses only past performance; even though it indicates nothing about future potential, useful inferences may be drawn from it. For example, if the market is competitively saturated and prospects for industry growth are limited, the strength or weakness of present market share is probably a key indicator of whether the business will be able to withstand and survive an industry shakeout.

Knowledge of Markets

Managers must first know their target markets. Who are the firm's customers? What is the demographic makeup of the target market and how is it changing? Perhaps most important, what are customer preferences and needs and how will these be changing in the future? Managers must also know their geographical market area. What changes or developments are occurring that may reflect on or affect the business? Is the demographic composition of the market area changing? Are important new competitors entering the market area? Managers must be aware of important market changes and directions. True, knowledge and awareness are intangible concepts and are susceptible to a wide range of interpretations. Yet this knowledge may be most critical in helping position a business to deal with future obstacles and opportunities.

Consider the case of Kultur International Films in Profile 6.3. Dennis Hedlund initially misread the target market for performing arts tapes. He attempted to market them to the general public rather than to the specific clientele interested in them. A more careful understanding of the appropriate target market enabled him to achieve his firm's potential.

Location

Although sometimes preestablished and unalterable, location dynamics can exert a significant impact on a business. In fact, poor location is generally listed as one of the primary reasons for the failure of retail businesses. Rating the relative strength of a location involves examining some rather obvious issues. A superb product or service may never be accepted if the business is in a bad location, but location may be a source of considerable strength if it provides visibility to the target market or clientele. For example, Atcom/Info is an emerging business capitalizing on the ever expanding need for information access. Recognizing that many business travelers don't carry laptop computers, Neil Senturia looked for a way to provide these travelers computer access for sending e-mail messages, checking stock prices, or tapping into other online sources. His idea was a public Internet kiosk, or Cyberbooth, the high-tech equivalent of a phone booth. Location became the key to his success. Senturia's company, Atcom, installed 167 high-speed Cyberbooths at airports, convention centers, and hotels—areas often frequented by business people.[1]

PROFILE 6.3

KULTUR INTERNATIONAL FILMS, LTD.

In the early 1980s, Dennis Hedlund conceived the idea of selling performing arts videos—operas, symphonies, ballets, and other high-brow material—through video stores. His company, Kulter International Films, Ltd., became the first company in the world to distribute performing arts programs on videocassettes. Starting with only two films featuring Arthur Rubenstein and Jascha Heifetz, Kulter made a corporate commitment to preserve on video the greatest performing artists of the 20th century for future generations to appreciate and enjoy. Kultur's historic programs include rare performances by Marian Anderson, Maria Callas, Mario Lanza, Billie Holiday, and many others.

Hedlund and his wife worked long hours trying to get video stores to buy the tapes. Hedlund even signed on as a sales representative for other video companies to gain access to video stores. Still, the stores wouldn't purchase his tapes. Store managers preferred to buy tapes of popular movies rather than stocking even a few performing arts videos. Finally, accepting that there simply wasn't a demand for the tapes in normal video stores, Hedlund began marketing the tapes through museums, dance studios, and art galleries. He also bought mailing lists and made special deals with fan clubs of the performers. He placed ads in specialty magazines catering to his particular target market. This marketing approach worked.

Today, Kultur is recognized as the leader in classical music video. He was even invited to Moscow at the height of the cold war to forge an agreement with the Soviet Union to distribute the cultural treasures of Russia into the West. Kultur's specialized marketing techniques were honored by *Inc.* and *Forbes* magazines when the company was placed on the list of the 500 fastest-growing American companies.

Kultur is selected by prestigious media companies around the world to distribute their programs on video. The Kultur catalog now contains over 1,000 programs, many of which have won Oscars,

Emmys, and film festival awards around the world. Kultur's new re-lease and production schedule is unmatched by any other studio or distributor in the industry. His plans for 1998 included over 100 pro-grams of, for example, new full-length ballets and operas, performing arts documentaries, and two new art series.

Kultur is positioned for strong growth well into the new century. The company's unique multifaceted ability to make available and effectively distribute the most desirable entertainment product in the world con-tinues to keep Kultur on its 18-year course of ever increasing growth and success.

Sources: www.kulturvideo.com, accessed May 28, 1998; and Jeffrey A. Tannenbaum, "Video Distributor Thrives at Last in Offering Culture." *The Wall Street Journal,* May 4, 1994, p. B2.

Location involves more than visibility. Other key factors include ease of access, availability of parking, traffic patterns, demographics, the com-plementary nature of neighboring businesses, and the location's image. Location image can often determine customers' reactions to and percep-tions of the business. For example, an upscale boutique located in a de-teriorated section of the community will probably not attract the desired clientele. Similarly, a family restaurant will be seriously and negatively affected if it is located in a high-crime area and buffered by bars on either side. The image of the location should support the desired image of the business.

Figure 6.8 lists a number of location factors for managers of a retail business to consider when expanding. You may want to add more. Figure 6.9 lists similar location factors that are important for growing manufac-turing businesses. Many of the factors that are critically important for re-tail businesses are of no concern to manufacturing businesses. For businesses such as those providing services, in which the business rep-resentative goes to customers' homes or offices, the specific location may be immaterial.

To use a matrix, create one that has factors on it that are critical to the business being analyzed. It is important, however, to create the matrix *before* performing the analysis. Once critical factors have been deter-mined, then analyze a number of locations. *Do not look for locations first.* If locations are found before managers determine the importance of cri-teria, managers tend to rationalize why a location is good or bad by

FIGURE 6.8 LOCATION FACTORS FOR RETAIL BUSINESSES

Factor	Excellent	Good	Fair	Poor
General location				
Proximity to customers				
Proximity to competitors				
Demographics of target market				
Size of building				
Size of parking lot				
Number of cars passing location				
Speed of cars passing location				
Distance from traffic signal				
Distance from corner				
Entrance/Exit				
Visibility distance				
Setback from street				
Placement of utilities, drainage, etc.				
Distance to nearest commercial neighbor				
Compatibility of commercial neighbors				

FIGURE 6.9 LOCATION FACTORS FOR MANUFACTURING BUSINESSES

Factor	Excellent	Good	Fair	Poor
General region				
Proximity to raw materials				
Proximity to transportation				
Types of available transportation				
Condition of available structures				
Zoning restrictions				
Tax rates				
Inducements from city				
Availability of utilities				
Availability of labor				

choosing criteria that influence the decision, and thus the objectivity provided by the matrices is lost. Only when the criteria are established first can the analysis be done with adequate objectivity.

Product

A firm's managers must evaluate the appeal of the products sold. Although products can be evaluated in absolute terms, the rating should also reflect the relative strength of products from a competitive perspective. Three product-related aspects should be considered: the product line, the attractiveness of the product, and the service provided with the product.

The product line refers to the variety of products the firm offers; and both the breadth and depth of the product line must be considered. A broad, or complete, line enables the business to meet a wide range of consumer needs; depth refers to the choices available within a product category. For example, one shoe store may offer a very narrow product line, limiting its business exclusively to shoes but offering a great number of styles and sizes. A competing store, presenting a broader product line, offers not only shoes but also an array of complementary or supportive products, such as polishes, socks, purses, and leather goods. Frequently, the store with the narrow line can still compete because of the depth of styles and sizes. The evaluation of product line must consider not only competitive influences but also the strategic approach the business is trying to promote. If the owner visualizes the company as a specialty business, its product line should reflect this strategy.

A second product-rating decision relates to the attractiveness of the firm's products. Here, managers need to view both product image and product quality from a consumer or market perspective. Purchases are made on the basis of perceived image and quality, even though the perceptions may be inconsistent with reality. If these perceptions are inaccurate, remedial action, perhaps in the form of advertising or promotion, can be used to help correct the misperceptions. Managers should strive to obtain an objective and unbiased evaluation of these factors. Often, outsiders may have to be consulted—small business managers are sometimes too close to their products to make an objective assessment.

Finally, managers must consider product service, which relates to the firm's assurances that consumer and product concerns will be effectively and fully addressed once sales have begun. Product warranties are important as are the number, availability, and quality of service representatives and service technicians.

Promotion

The promotions mix for a company consists of its personal selling, advertising, publicity, and sales promotion. The strength of a company's promotion efforts needs to be evaluated; and objective evidence of the effectiveness of these efforts is available in some situations. For example, a business may note sales growth following certain advertising campaigns. Often, however, such information is not available, making promotion one of the most difficult areas to assess. Most managers realize the significance of reaching consumers, informing them of the company's products, and encouraging them to make purchases. Overall advertising and other promotional emphases, however, are hard to analyze from an objective and competitive perspective. This is one reason managers often feel that advertising and promotion is one of the most expendable resources: The advertising and promotion budget is one of the first to be reduced or eliminated when the small business encounters financial strains. Ironically, this is often precisely the wrong strategic decision.

To evaluate the firm's promotion activities, managers must have a feel for how important these factors are to the industry in which the business operates. If competitors in the industry rely heavily on advertising to generate sales, for example, then meager and ineffective advertising and promotion may be a significant weakness. However, if industry sales are driven by a few established and regular contract sales, large investments in advertising and promotion may be unnecessary. It may be useful to compare the firm's expenditures for advertising and promotion with those typical of the industry and with those of immediate competitors. If competitors are investing heavily in advertising, a similar response may be necessary to keep or gain market share. Trade associations are helpful in determining industry trends or norms with which a company's promotional efforts may be compared.

In some industries, personal selling is the key to success. This is especially true in business-to-business selling and in some service businesses. Even in retail businesses, the sales force must be analyzed. Personal selling can be studied by looking at sales per salesperson, sales per department, or sales per product line.

Even publicity can be studied. A company can get free publicity in a number of ways—working for charitable causes that might do a press release noting contributions, sending news items to local newspapers, offering to be interviewed as "experts" in a human interest broadcast on television, and holding contests for prizes. Such efforts should not be done randomly but should be carefully planned to get the most return for the effort.

Price

Price should reflect the strategy or image the business wants to project. A discount store, for example, makes a statement with its low prices, but managers stressing quality, service, or exclusivity often set high prices to reflect a higher image.

The strength or weakness of a pricing strategy is strongly influenced by the competition. An owner may set prices based on costs (for raw materials, assembly, sales expenses, and others) and be unable to lower them to realize an acceptable return; but if a key competitor lowers its prices, the firm's inability to respond accordingly may be viewed as a price weakness. On the other hand, price may be rated a definite strength when size of operations, economies of scale, and production efficiency enable a business to offer products at consistently lower prices than the competition.

Image

Image has both internal and external ramifications. That is, the image of the business is reflected through its internal culture or climate and in that way affects the employees; and, in addition, the image is perceived by those outside the business and affects their attitudes toward the business. The image should be consistent with the strategies of the business, in which case image emerges as an important strength. Otherwise, image can be a weakness. If a business wishes to stress personal service as a competitive factor, for example, it should present an image reflecting openness, concern for workers, communication, and trust. If quality is being stressed, an image of high skill, training, and attention to detail is valuable.

Image evolves as the firm continues in operation. The public's perception of the firm's image is based on the historical exposure of the public to the business. Past mistakes, missed deadlines, and arrogant previous owners may all be to blame. Clearly, these perceptions may not be the fault of present owners, and present conditions may suggest an image drastically different from the common public view. If this is the case, the present owners need to recognize image as a problem area and create changes in the public's perception of it. Because changes tend to be incremental, remember that image definitely affects customer attitudes toward the business and, in turn, the consumption pattern of customers.

Image is, unfortunately, difficult to measure, depending largely on such informal measures as complaints (or lack of complaints), word of mouth, and recommendations from satisfied customers. Because image directly affects future customers, simply watching the type of customer that comes through the door can indicate the effectiveness of the image message. No matter what image is sought, entrepreneurs and managers must direct all their actions toward presenting that image.

Distribution

Are the channels of distribution accessible and acceptable? Does the product flow from the business to consumers in a reasonable and cost-effective way? In many cases, the firm's product reaches the ultimate consumer only after passing through a set of intermediaries: A manufacturer may distribute directly to retailers or to a wholesaler, who in turn sells to a number of retailers, or to both retailers and wholesalers. Each stage of the distribution process may need to be evaluated to gain a clear notion of the relative strength of the entire system.

Analyzing distribution for a product-manufacturing firm should consider everything from the point at which the product comes off the assembly line to the point when the final user receives the product. This may include warehousing, inventory policies, shipping methods, and billing.

Two factors are important in analyzing distribution: cost and coverage. The two factors tend to work against each other. A manufacturing firm, for example, may find that it is cheaper to distribute products directly to customers, but only a few customers can be reached. By using intermediaries such as wholesalers and retailers, added cost is incurred but significant increases in market coverage can be achieved. Often in these cases, the cost of the intermediaries is far outweighed by the increase in coverage.

Few measures are available to indicate that distribution is being done well, but there are sometimes indications that it is being done poorly. Products sitting in the loading dock area for an excessive amount of time, for example, indicate poor distribution. "Stockouts" among retail stores, even though the manufacturing plant is not overworked, is another indication of problems with distribution. And if the cost of distribution seems out of line, the area needs to be studied.

EVALUATING OPERATIONAL RESOURCES

Operational resources are those that are involved with or that support the production of a product or service. They may relate to the physical elements of a job or to relationships within the business and with key contacts outside the business. Clearly, relevant resources are numerous, but five key areas must be evaluated: production facilities, access to suppliers, inventory control, organization structure, and quality control.

Production Facilities

Production facilities should be viewed broadly, and a number of issues should be considered when rating these facilities. First, the firm's existing plant and equipment must be evaluated. Is the physical plant large enough to handle the desired scope of business operations? Has the business made the technical advances in plant and equipment necessary to remain competitive? Is the equipment used by the business technically and operationally sound and efficient?

Part of this analysis should address the issue of capacity. Is the business operating near capacity or significantly below capacity? Either condition could be viewed as a potential weakness depending on the growth projections of the business. Further, the physical layout and work flow must be evaluated. Do the production facilities permit work to be arranged in the most efficient and productive manner?

Access to Suppliers

Of the two basic questions that emerge here, the first concerns basic availability. Does the business have ready access to necessary raw materials and suppliers? The second question concerns the cost considerations that must temper availability. How much do materials and supplies cost? A promising opportunity may be hurt by either costly or inconsistent sources of supply.

Managers of growing manufacturing companies must determine whether to purchase their inventory of components from a single supplier or a number of different suppliers. This problem is made worse if the industry as a whole is also rapidly growing, in which case availability of components may be a continuing problem. Some manufacturers rely on strategic alliances with suppliers to ensure the availability of quality products. Other manufacturers may go a step further and actually buy their supplier in order to control the availability of products.

Retailers have an especially close dependence on suppliers. Managers must carefully consider that relationship because customers may depend on the retailer to purchase specific brands of products. Changing brand selection or suppliers may adversely affect customer relations. Service businesses typically are not as tied to suppliers as are retailers or manufacturers, but managers of service businesses should still look at the relationship with suppliers as part of an overall internal analysis.

Potential entrepreneurs must carefully assess supplier relations before beginning their business. If suppliers can't be relied on, the entrepreneur must weigh that risk against the alternative of using other, perhaps more expensive, suppliers or even not starting the business at all. In one previously mentioned case, a candy retailer had to completely close down after a key supplier couldn't meet the retailer's needs.

Inventory Control

In examining inventory, a manager evaluates the strength of the system for stocking, ordering, and reordering materials (raw or finished products). Success in this area may be the key to meeting customers' needs on time. Does the manager know what materials are on hand? Can they be located and accessed? Are there clear, established procedures for initiating reorders? Is there usually an acceptable level of materials in stock, or is the business regularly plagued with inventory backlogs and outages? For start-up companies, an inventory control system may not need to be computerized or highly sophisticated, but it should prompt action that will ensure steady, desired inventory flows. As a business grows, however, the inventory control system may need to become automated, ranging from a simple spreadsheet-type program to a completely automated bar-coding system that electronically places an order with suppliers' computer-based ordering systems when inventory reaches a certain level.

The emerging business faces an inventory dilemma: Needed inventory must be on hand so that production runs are not hampered and customers are not frustrated at production delays, but inventory holding costs can be quite formidable. Therefore, the emerging business tries to limit inventory to the basic level it needs to maintain a consistent flow of operations, an option provided by the popular just-in-time (JIT) inventory system. Under the JIT system, the supplier delivers components when, where, and in the quantities needed. Of course, a JIT system is only as effective as the relationship and communication that exists between the business and its suppliers. Automated information systems are essential, so all of the factors discussed here may need to be weighed when evaluating the system of inventory control.

The need for inventory control goes far beyond simply counting inventory. In a high-growth market, a firm's managers may decide to produce components themselves rather than risk unreliable suppliers. On the other hand, managing substantial amounts of inventory is expensive in addition to the internal cost of producing the products in-house. New businesses are often well advised to outsource everything possible to reduce the fixed cost of plant and equipment necessary to produce components in-house.

Structure

The structure of an organization is the formal flow of information and authority within it, indicating the jobs that people do and accompanying areas of responsibility. The organizational structure should be consistent with and support the strategies and objectives of the business. If the business desires operational flexibility, an informal or open structural system may be preferable. The key to evaluating the structure is to note if the business and its personnel are restricted by the demands of the structure or if the structure is logical and helps employees fulfill their responsibilities.

Managers of new and growing firms will often choose to structure the business around functional areas, that is, marketing, finance, accounting, human resources, and operations. Others may want to build the structure around particular products. Still others, especially service businesses, may want to structure around particular key customers. The important part of this analysis is to determine whether the structure is as efficient as possible while still allowing the company to achieve its objectives.

A problem that is unique to emerging businesses is the need to change or adjust the structure to accommodate the growth of the business. Indicators of inefficiencies in structure are miscommunication, delays in getting authority to implement new ideas, problems in dealing with customers, employee complaints, and defects in products. If the problems are indeed caused by an inappropriate structure, solutions may include restructuring around key customers, key products, or key processes to become more attentive to priority areas in the business.

Quality Control

Managers of any business must evaluate the policies and procedures that the organization uses to ensure the quality of its products and services. We live in an era when business is held to ever rising quality standards. In fact, quality is one of the strongest explanations for the long-term success of a business in today's competitive environment. The assessment of quality is especially important for both new and emerging businesses because both are vulnerable during start-up and growth phases. Because managers' attention will be distracted by the demands of start-up or growth, quality may slip because of inattention. Thus, special efforts must be made to assess quality and ensure that it receives adequate emphasis.

Although quality may be assessed from many perspectives, users of a firm's goods and services often offer the most important signals. Customers and clients provide excellent evidence of their satisfaction with quality by their reactions to the products and services they receive. For example, if the business provides components for a large industrial manufacturer, quality specifications are normally designated contractually. Failure to meet these standards may mean losing the contract. On the other hand, if the business serves a retail or service market, customer complaints or product returns may signal quality deficiencies.

Managers, however, should not assume that quality is acceptable simply because customer complaints are not being heard—unacceptable quality may be reflected in decreased sales. A slip in quality is often difficult to detect, and quality comparisons between competitors are often quite subjective and subtle. Therefore, specific procedures must be enacted to detect quality concerns. Some businesses, for example, rely on customer surveys to find potential quality problems, whereas others conduct regular internal audits to spot problem areas. Whatever set of procedures is used, quality assessment is a critical factor in internal analysis.

EVALUATING HUMAN RESOURCES

The final category of internal factors that should be analyzed is a firm's human resources. Although this component is often overlooked, a firm's employees may be one of its most critical assets. We view human resources broadly to include all employees of the firm along with their unique skills and abilities.

An initial concern for new businesses is to examine the number of employees required and the relevancy of their skills. An entrepreneur may be tempted to either overstaff or understaff a new business either because of grandiose plans or a too limited vision of the firm's potential. Another fault that is typical of an entrepreneur is to hire friends or relatives. Unfortunately, this is often done without regard to the relevant skills each possesses, and, as a result, the entrepreneur is often faced later with firing those same friends or relatives because they don't share the entrepreneur's vision for the company. It is better for the entrepreneur to carefully consider the real needs of the new company and select employees accordingly.

Similarly, managers of growth-oriented businesses must determine how many employees are needed and what specific skills are required to make possible the desired growth. If required skills are missing, the firm must either train existing employees or hire additional workers who have the necessary skills. As the business grows, human resource planning can become quite complex. This is especially true for companies that are growing rapidly; the manager often can't hire new employees fast enough to support the growing business. It is tempting for emerging business managers to want to personally hire each new employee, but that is a time-consuming process. The manager must soon realize that the recruiting and hiring process has to be delegated to others.

A second human resource consideration is the assessment of employee morale and management-labor relations. Morale is a key factor yet fairly difficult to measure accurately. In most situations, the business need not take the time and effort to conduct a formal morale survey; a set of more informal indicators may suffice. Employee turnover, absenteeism, tardiness, and a general assessment of the workday climate should provide a notion of morale. Frequent grumblings, complaints, arguments, and conflicts may indicate weakened morale. Again, an attempt should be made to ascertain a general feeling about morale as it affects business action. Morale should never be ignored—a poorly motivated and uncommitted workforce can undermine a well-focused growth strategy.

Although morale is important in any business, it is especially important in a new business or one embarking on a concerted growth strategy, where the morale and cohesiveness of employees is critical. In these two situations managers must depend heavily on employees to carry their share of the load and more. Often, long hours are required to keep the business going. Employees with good morale are usually willing to put in that extra effort, even if the pay is less than that in competing firms. But poor morale results in employees unwilling to put out extra effort and who may have to be cajoled into working at a productive level. Poor morale certainly can slow down the work process and can sometimes be severe enough that a growth strategy may have to be abandoned completely.

A third factor to examine is the business's compensation system—that is, wages and salary plus any fringe benefits. For our purposes the essential determinations are whether the present compensation system is (1) adequate and (2) consistent with the strategic direction of the firm.

The adequacy of a firm's compensation is determined by both internal and external comparisons. Internally, most workers will feel compensation is adequate if it is distributed equitably; that is, better performers earn more than lesser performers. However, if considerable work is being done in teams, team members must feel their compensation is fair in relation to one another. Indeed, an internal perception that compensation is equitable is key to employee motivation and the credibility of the compensation system. Externally, adequacy of compensation is largely a function of competition. Are workers receiving compensation that is reasonably consistent with that of workers in similar firms and industries?

Workers may be willing to accept a lower salary if other factors make up for it. Suppose, for example, that two businesses are competing for the same labor market. One provides a slightly higher compensation package, but the second offers a more challenging, interesting, and pleasant work environment. Some workers may feel that the opportunities available at the second business outweigh the compensation difference. But managers should not deceive themselves. In general, workers expect compensation that is similar to, or better than, that of competitors.

The compensation system must also be consistent with the strategic thrust of the firm. If the firm is moving aggressively into new markets and depending on the efforts of its sales force to attract new customers, the compensation system must reflect this dependence. Quotas, bonuses, or a commission system may be needed to motivate workers to attract new contacts and businesses. The firm's hourly wage may have worked fine in the past, but new demands require new motivational efforts.

When compensation is discussed, it is usual to assume that the focus is on dollars. Yet much compensation is nonmonetary; such things as office furnishings, company cars, vacation scheduling, and more interpersonal issues can also affect the motivation of employees. For example, the willingness of managers to allow employees to adjust their working hours may have an impact on motivation. If managers are attempting to build a unified, loyal workforce with a strong commitment to the business, then companywide performance incentives may be appropriate. A properly designed system can help the manager achieve desired results.

A final human resource area that should be assessed is training. Here the question to be answered is whether employees are receiving the training necessary to do their jobs well. Training can be either in-house or off-site. It can be either technical training on how to use new software programs or classes on team building. Training should be ongoing as long as it does not unduly interrupt the actual work of the business. Managers should have an eye open for indications of the need for training.

One area in which training is important in today's businesses is technology. Computers and software change so rapidly that it's difficult to keep up with new developments. Sometimes sending people to half-day or full-day workshops yields productivity far in excess of attempts to train employees in new processes during normal workdays.

THE CONSULTANT'S VIEWPOINT

Our list of internal areas or factors to be analyzed is by no means all-inclusive but merely is intended to provide a general framework for those beginning the process of internal analysis. Starting the internal analysis with a general framework is critical. Quite often, managers from small businesses to Fortune 100 companies attempt to perform comprehensive internal analyses by simply attending a half-day retreat to "brainstorm." While this approach may provide creative insights into sources of strengths and weaknesses, when used alone it may also expose a firm to unnecessary risks. When managers simply brainstorm to analyze their internal operations, they may overlook critical sources of competitive strengths or weaknesses. A specified methodology can ensure that they cover all their bases when performing an internal analysis. Using a general framework during an internal analysis will decrease the possibility of getting blindsided by missing a source of critical strength or weakness.

Clearly, there is no single approach that applies to every organization. Therefore, it will be necessary to select those items that are most relevant to the particular situation, perhaps evaluating areas other than those noted in this chapter. Or the list can be a condensed version of what is presented here. As a company and its managers become more experienced with the strategic planning process, the internal analysis should become more focused and specific to the needs and demands of the business. Managers will soon learn which factors are key indicators to the business and analyze these factors in greater depth.

Future-Oriented Framework

This chapter may help those interested in assessing the current position of a firm, but the focus of the book is strategic planning. More important than a firm's current position, therefore, is a firm's position in relation to its future ability to compete and its ability to achieve long-term corporate goals.

We are interested in a firm's current financial position, but we are more interested in its capability to embark on a new strategy given its current position. We may determine that the distribution system is adequate. But when we consider that we may be expanding next year, then the distribution system may not be adequate. The morale in a manufacturing plant may be acceptable, but will it still be after we make major changes in the manufacturing process? The focus must be on the future.

Externally Driven Perspective

As noted in previous chapters, strategic planning is an externally driven process. Therefore, it is imperative that external conditions are sufficiently understood before a firm starts its internal analysis. Quite often, firms will look inward in an attempt to identify strengths and weaknesses. Remember, though, it's not the firm that determines strengths and weaknesses—it's the market.

Consider, for example, a firm that embarks on the internal analysis process by looking inward rather than looking outward at the external environment. Managers of the firm may conclude that their reputation for stability is a core strength for the company, so the company decides to invest considerable resources to further develop this perceived strength. Suppose, however, that customers in this firm's market aren't concerned at all with a reputation for stability. They aren't loyal to any one firm because their only concern is getting the product for the lowest possible price. In such a case, the firm is investing resources in something that the market doesn't consider important. Not only is the firm wasting time on something that doesn't improve its competitive position, but financial resources may be misallocated rather than being invested in something that would benefit the company's long-term success.

DISCUSSION QUESTIONS

1. Should external analysis be done before internal analysis? Why or why not?
2. Why is collecting accurate data about the "people" part of the business difficult?
3. How do you decide which areas to analyze first and in how much depth?
4. Choose a company that you know well. Perform an internal analysis, including the following:
   a. Financial analysis
   b. Analysis of the strengths and weaknesses related to marketing
   c. Analysis of the efficiency of the firm's operations
   d. Analysis of the human resources of the company, assuming low growth and then assuming high growth
5. What would likely be key internal factors for the following businesses? Will your answer be the same for each of them?
   a. a research engineering firm
   b. a manufacturer of computer printers
   c. a food wholesaler
   d. a retailer of cellular phones

NOTES

1. Shaifali Puri, "Cool Companies," *Fortune,* July 7, 1997, pp. 87–88.

CHAPTER 7

RECOGNIZING DISTINCTIVE COMPETENCIES AND COMPETITIVE WEAKNESSES

C hapters 4, 5, and 6 detail the process of analyzing the external environment and the internal strengths and weaknesses of a company, with stress on the importance and relevance of careful analysis. Those chapters focus on data gathering and analysis and address what things we should consider, how to gather information, and how to analyze information to reach conclusions. This chapter considers the final step in the analysis phase of our model—recognizing distinctive competencies and competitive weaknesses. The chapter blends the external and internal analysis, allowing managers to take advantage of the company's strengths and offset its weaknesses. Considering distinctive competencies and competitive weaknesses is necessary when crafting the company's strategies. After studying this chapter, you should be able to

- define distinctive competencies;
- understand how to develop a strength into a distinctive competence;
- realize the importance of a sustainable competence; and
- recognize the difference between a weakness and a significant competitive weakness.

129

ENVIRONMENTAL OPPORTUNITIES VERSUS RELEVANT BUSINESS OPPORTUNITIES

Analyzing the relevant external environment will likely reveal a number of possible areas of opportunity. Perhaps competitors have become so big they no longer provide the personal touch that consumers have come to desire and expect. Perhaps new segments or niches in the market are appearing but have not been targeted. Perhaps consumer needs and preferences are shifting so that adding complementary products or services will significantly increase sales and profits.

Merely identifying opportunities, however, does not mean that a firm either can or should take advantage of these opportunities. This determination is made after carefully considering the internal analysis. For example, changing demographic and social factors within a given community may suggest that a restaurant–dinner theater combination is an attractive opportunity. Suppose there is no dinner theater in the community and the increasing population base of young, upscale consumers seems likely to support one. A particular restaurant in the community may accurately recognize this as an environmental opportunity. But internal analysis clearly reveals that the restaurant has neither the employees nor the financial resources to commit to such a project, so the environmental opportunity can't be translated into a relevant business opportunity. Environmental opportunities only become relevant business opportunities when an internal analysis reveals that a business is able to capitalize on these opportunities.

The distinction between environmental opportunities and business opportunities is critical for emerging businesses. Care must be taken to make sure growth opportunities are, in fact, the best areas of growth that the business should pursue. This can only occur through a thorough understanding of the firm's internal condition. Successful growth requires a careful mesh between opportunities and capacities.

While perhaps less obvious, new ventures face similar issues. Entrepreneurs, for example, must determine whether resources are sufficient to pursue new competitive options. Indeed, one of the most insightful responses owners and managers of new ventures may make is to back away from some environmental opportunities. In some cases, pursuing opportunities—even seemingly promising opportunities—may drain resources to the point that the business is simply spread too thin.

A company's managers may be able to identify a number of environmental opportunities. In general, the more dynamic and growth oriented an industry, the greater the number of environmental opportunities. Similarly, the more open, responsive, and financially sound a business is, the greater the number of relevant business opportunities it is likely to realize.

The distinction between environmental opportunities and relevant business opportunities may be somewhat arbitrary or subjective; yet it is critical to strategic planning. A business must be concerned with acting on those opportunities that have survived the scrutiny of internal analysis and become relevant business opportunities.

THE ROLE OF DISTINCTIVE COMPETENCIES

A distinctive competence is any area, factor, or consideration that gives a business a meaningful competitive edge. Distinctive competencies—activities that a firm not only does well but does better than all other competitors—positively distinguish a firm from its competitors. Distinctive competencies may include superior products, brand loyalty, or technological know-how. They may even include processes used by a firm such as ISO 9000 certification or an effective just-in-time inventory control system. Distinctive competencies often emerge and grow as managers position a firm to enhance its competitive position.[1] Consider the case of Amazon.com that is presented in Profile 7.1. Started in July 1995 as an online store, Amazon.com is a rapidly emerging business. Along the way, it has carefully crafted a distinctive competence: It has found a unique niche in a highly competitive industry by capitalizing on available technology and consumers' growing need for convenience.

IDENTIFYING AND DEVELOPING AREAS OF DISTINCTIVE COMPETENCE

Distinctive competencies may appear in either of two ways. One way is their appearance as part of a firm's current operations. As the business exists over time, it operates in such a manner that clear and important competencies are present, perhaps having initially arisen out of the firm's mission or managerial orientation. Over time, they become an integral part of the business. Courtland Clubs (Profile 7.2) is an example.

PROFILE 7.1

Amazon.Com

Hey, let's go browse in a bookstore. How about Amazon.com? OK, have a seat and turn on your computer.

Amazon.com is not your father's bookstore. It is also not your local Barnes & Noble, Borders, or Crown. But if you ask many people where they buy their books, you'll soon hear someone mention Amazon.com.

Amazon.com is a virtual bookstore. Located in a downtown Seattle office building, books are nowhere in view. Amazon actually stocks a few hundred high-demand titles, and these are in a warehouse somewhere in Seattle, but Amazon.com can get you almost any book in print. (Even this book is available.) Some books will be shipped in 24 hours; some require two to four days. Browsing the Amazon.com Web site without ordering at least one book takes discipline indeed. It's as simple as entering your credit card number and your address, dropping the book in the "shopping cart," and clicking "order." If you have a book in mind, you can type in the title. If you have a subject in mind (such as strategic planning) you type that in and click "search." There's more. How about a contest? Perhaps you'd like a review of a popular book by either a critic or a customer. Even authors can comment on their own works. And if you find a book you like, you'll also find a list of other books that people have bought in addition to the one you're considering.

Amazon.com's sales went from zero to $15.7 million in 1996 and in the first quarter of 1997 hit $16 million. Amazon went public in 1997 at slightly under $20 a share. By mid-1998, its stock had been as high as 100.

Source: Charles C. Mann, "Volume Business," *Inc. Technology,* no. 2 (June 17, 1997): 54–61; Amazon.com Web site www.amazon.com, accessed May 27, 1998.

PROFILE 7.2

COURTLAND CLUBS

Courtland Clubs was an established tennis club in a medium-sized metropolitan location. It had been in business for more than 25 years and had prided itself on the quality and aesthetics of both its indoor and outdoor courts. Although its prices were high, the club had attracted a prosperous, upscale clientele and had experienced steady growth. Courtland Clubs had developed a reputation as the "in" club among the business and professional community. To a large extent, the social climate of the club was more important to its members than were athletic opportunities.

In the early 1990s, Courtland's management team became aware that cross-training and a variety of physical activity options were becoming more significant to its target market than the socialization factor had been in the past. The management team feared that membership might start to dip because many members viewed the club from a social perspective.

In analyzing its environment, Courtland recognized numerous growth opportunities—becoming a health club complete with weight machines and general workout equipment; adding racquetball facilities; installing an indoor running track; and offering year-round aerobic workouts. Courtland had the staff, land, and physical and financial resources to capitalize on any or all of these possibilities, but other clubs were already providing these features, and it appeared that the last thing the community needed, or could support, was another health and exercise club. Courtland's owners felt they had responded too slowly to environmental shifts and new consumer needs and were thus stuck in a losing situation.

The management team assembled to discuss the problem. One of them asked, "Is there any way we can compete in the health club, racquetball, and running club areas given the present level of competitive saturation?" The answer was perhaps, if the Courtland design was unique or special enough to attract users from existing clubs to its fa-cilities. But how were they to build such a club?

The answer lay in the distinctive competencies that Courtland had so carefully nurtured over its 25-year existence—quality facilities, luxu-ries, and a competent and helpful staff that catered to the wishes of its unique (and growing) target market. With this competency in mind, the owners were able to devise a strategic plan and direction and enlarge its offerings.

In its competitive situation, Courtland needed to recognize its areas of competence, determine whether they were still viable, and then pro-ceed to use them as the focus for evaluating environmental opportunities and strategic direction.

In some situations, however, distinctive competencies may need to be developed or nurtured—particularly if none currently exist, as is the case with new businesses. Entrepreneurs analyze the competitive envi-ronment, scrutinize internal resources, and carefully and objectively de-cide which areas are most fruitful for development. In this approach, the one Amazon.com pursued to a large extent, managers attempt to build areas of competence.

Such a building or development process can be quite trying for both new and emerging small businesses. Essentially, managers should inves-tigate areas where they can create a meaningful competence, realizing that the competitive environment, the firm's internal capacities, and the firm's reactions within its competitive environment dictate competen-cies. Consider the case of cybercafes (Profile 7.3) that purposefully iden-tify an area of competitive uniqueness and commit energy and resources to develop it. This area becomes a distinctive competence because it meets the needs of today's fast-paced, connected society.

In spite of the difficulty in compiling an exhaustive set of competen-cies, Figure 7.1 lists nine of the more common areas of distinctive com-petence likely to be recognized by emerging small businesses.

Quality is a key area of competence and one that is of growing im-portance to consumers. Here, a business offers consumers a product or service that is of discernibly higher quality than the quality offered by the competition. Accordingly, consumers come to associate a quality image with the business.

PROFILE 7.3

Cybercafes: Coffee, Computers, and Comaraderie

Coffee cafes are the rage today. Apparently, people encountering the hustle-bustle lifestyle of the late 1990s find relaxation in the casual, customer-focused style of these shops. The downside, particularly from a business perspective, is the omnipresence of the shops—they're seemingly everywhere—with little to distinguish one from another. True, Starbucks has a strategy as it has coupled its operations with Barnes & Noble Booksellers, but how do others compete and create a meaningful distinctive competence? The answer—a cybercafe!

Webolution Café in Albuquerque, WWW Café Inc. in Austin, and Bean Central in Nashville have all created a unique style for their shops. They offer Internet access that allows customers to check their e-mail while sipping their morning brew. The online charges vary from shop to shop; for example, Webolution charges $4 for a half-hour hookup. Customers now seek out these shops rather than those without such clever technological options.

The commonality among cybercafes is their distinctive competence that they created through a mix of coffee, computers, and camaraderie.

Source: Danielle Reed, "Takeoffs & Landings," *The Wall Street Journal,* April 24, 1998, p. W7.

Service often moves hand-in-hand with quality and refers to a business's efforts to aid consumers in their dealings with the business and its products. The efforts to provide service may occur before a sale or when repairs and follow-up are needed after a sale.

Location is a factor that often dictates a firm's success and can be an area of considerable competence when recognized and exploited. Location may affect a firm's visibility, its likelihood of attracting the target market, and its competitive edge over businesses offering similar products or services.

FIGURE 7.1   AREAS OF DISTINCTIVE COMPETENCE COMMONLY
RECOGNIZED BY EMERGING SMALL BUSINESSES

Quality	Strong consumer orientation
Service	Reputation and image
Location	Personnel
Filling a special niche	Price
Flexibility and adaptability	

Filling a special niche is a particularly important competence and one that can be developed after careful analysis of the competitive situation. A business may choose to enter an untapped market, provide unique services or products (and thus limit direct competition), or add aspects of novelty or originality to existing products. Such extensions and variations must be focused on real needs of some segment of the market, however. Providing a unique product that no one cares about or wants to purchase is counterproductive.

Flexibility and adaptability may be particular strengths an emerging small business can focus on that offer it a competitive edge over larger, more formalized, and more rigid operations. For example, an emerging business may do custom work and thereby attract customers from larger firms who don't offer custom services.

A strong consumer orientation is often promoted by smaller businesses, which, perhaps because of a less formalized, bureaucratic process, are able to stay in closer touch with shifting consumer needs and demands and respond more quickly to them. Consumers are likely to feel that a company's employees know them and are willing to adapt and modify their methods and operations to accommodate customers' individuality.

Reputation and image may be a function of a number of other areas, yet consumers often see their cumulative effect in a general or encompassing way.

Personnel can be an area of competence when managers and other employees have extensive experience or knowledge, factors that are business strengths. When customers recognize these strengths and believe they are superior, a distinctive competence exists. For example, two large grocery stores both have experienced, knowledgeable workers. One store, however, is primarily self-service where customers place their own groceries on the checkout conveyor and then sack them after they pay. The second store emphasizes personal interaction and help; employees sack the groceries, and the front of the carts opens at the level of the scanner so customers don't have to unload the cart. Both stores possess employee-related strengths, but only the second has transferred that strength into a distinctive competency.

Finally, *price,* which is often stressed, is a tenuous competency—powerful yet remarkably fragile. Its potential as a competency may be significant if competitors are conservative and new entrants into the market are unlikely. However, if a competitor is willing or able to alter its existing price structure, this competency can be stripped of its value very quickly. Price is therefore often viewed as a rather short-term competency.

These nine areas are competencies only if a firm's customers perceive them as such. Perception is often more important than reality. Managers may correctly feel that the firm's customer service is superior to that of the immediate competition, but service is not a distinctive competency if customers don't perceive it as different from, and better than, that of competitors. Service is at best an unexploited strength, for a strength must be built or developed into a true area of distinctive competence. Effectively marketing a strength may be the bridge to creating a distinctive competency.

RELATING DISTINCTIVE COMPETENCIES TO RELEVANT BUSINESS OPPORTUNITIES

Not all environmental opportunities are relevant business opportunities, as noted earlier, and not all business opportunities should be exploited. Which relevant business opportunities should an emerging business choose to pursue? In general, management will select business opportunities in those areas where they possess some unique or special advantage over competitors. In other words, a business should focus on opportunities for which it has distinctive competencies.

The significance of this point is often overlooked or misunderstood. Managers frequently believe that if a relevant business opportunity is present, they should try to capitalize on it even though it may be a poor use of the firm's resources. For example, a number of competitors may be about to respond to the same opportunity, and some of these competitors may be better able to do so. To commit to an area in which a firm is, from the outset, at a definite competitive disadvantage is poor business sense. Areas in which a business possesses a meaningful competitive edge over its competitors are the areas that should be emphasized.

In addition, leaders of new and emerging businesses must be sure that pursuing new opportunities will not threaten the main mission and focus of the business. In other words, an opportunity may exist and the business may have the capacity to act on it, but its managers may decide that doing so threatens the business in some important way.

Consider the case of Primordial, makers of Zobo—brightly colored plastic linking toys that resemble genetic strands of DNA when assembled. In the company's early years, it faced a most tempting opportunity when asked to include its product in the marketing efforts for the movie *The Lost World,* the sequel to *Jurassic Park.* Reasoning that such a move would link their toy forever in customer's minds as a *Jurassic Park* spin-off, Primordial's founders opted against this strategy despite its short-run promise. Instead, they emphasized their focus of making their own brand, with its own distinct image and special approach to marketing. The opportunity offered by *The Lost World* could have potentially clouded this focus and harmed the long-run growth of the business.[2]

SUSTAINABLE COMPETENCIES

It is one thing to have or develop a distinctive competence. It is quite another to maintain it. The more successful a company is because of a competence, the more competitors will attempt to imitate or improve on it. Anything a manager can do to sustain a competence and prevent competitors from encroaching on its territory will go far in ensuring success for the business. Actions that can sustain a competence include patenting a product or process, keeping formulas for products secret, advertising the product heavily to develop brand loyalty, and developing unique containers and catchy slogans or product names that encourage customers to identify with the particular product or company. Clearly, tangible resources as a source of distinctive competence are much easier to imitate compared with intangible resources or capabilities as a source of distinctive competence.

Ben & Jerry's Homemade Ice Cream, Inc., is an example of a company that has worked hard to sustain its areas of competence. The flavors of its superpremium, high-fat, expensive ice cream carry such exotic names as Cherry Garcia, Rainforest Crunch, New York Super Fudge Chunk, White Russian, Chubby Hubby, and Coconut Almond Fudge Chip. The company also publicizes its adamant commitment to social causes. Many customers buy Ben & Jerry's ice cream partially because of the good taste and catchy names and partially because of the company's reputation for involvement in social causes.

Some companies, such as Columbia Sportswear, shown in Profile 7.4, go to great lengths to protect their competencies. The press release from Columbia Sportswear illustrates the effort it goes to in protecting its designs.

Few competencies are sustainable forever. Even IBM, previously the epitome of success in the computer industry, fell on hard times in the early 1990s before rebounding in the mid-1990s. Declining sales occur repeatedly among real estate companies in medium-sized cities. For a few years, one company dominates the community's sale of real estate; a few years later, another firm leads the pack; still later, another will take over as number one. A real estate firm is able to ward off competitors for a few years because of its size or because its key executives are well known in the city. The success of that firm, however, eventually fades when a competitor tries some other approach that customers find appealing. The tenuous nature of distinctive competencies should prompt managers to search for ways to sustain their competencies.

DISTINCTIVE COMPETENCIES AND STRATEGIC PLANNING

The determination or recognition of a firm's distinctive competencies is one of the critical, culminating events of the analysis phase of strategic planning. The distinctive competencies of the business become the focus or driving force behind selecting relevant business opportunities, preparing mission and goal statements, and planning strategic actions.

It may be useful to refine the steps or processes that make up the analysis phase of the strategic planning model (see Figure 7.2). First, environmental analysis yields a series of environmental opportunities, which are then subjected to the scrutiny of internal analysis to determine if they are in fact relevant business opportunities. Additional analysis focusing on competitors and key internal strengths permits a firm to clearly recognize its distinctive competencies (or pinpoint those most fruitful for development). Then, relevant business opportunities are evaluated in terms of a recognized distinctive competence. Those opportuni-

PROFILE 7.4

Columbia Sportswear Forges Ahead in Battle against Trademark Infringers

Portland, Ore. (December 5, 1997) Fervently protecting its products and brand image worldwide, active outdoor clothing and footwear giant Columbia Sportswear Company® has forced California apparel manufacturer Moose Creed to stop selling copies of its popular Half Moon Short™. The Half Moon Short, a technical angling short, is part of Columbia's Performance Fishing Gear collection.

Moose Creek's Safari Short so closely resembled the Half Moon Short that Columbia felt its brand image and potentially sales of the Half Moon Short would have been compromised. Moose Creek agreed to immediately cancel production on its Safari Short. "Columbia Sportswear has become a particularly attractive target for trademark infringers because our products perform so well at retail," said company President and Chief Executive Officer Tim Boyle. "As we forge ahead in our international expansion, it is imperative that we preserve our brand image and product integrity, so we will continue to use every legal measure to protect our trade dress rights from those who try to profit from our expertise."

Columbia's trade dress rights arise from its unique designs being so distinctive that they identify the company as the source of the product. Columbia employees, independent sales representatives, and distributors all over the world are trained to identify and intercept knockoffs, and to immediately report them to corporate headquarters. Over the past five years, Columbia has successfully halted more than 40 companies in four countries from selling knockoffs of its popular outerwear.

Columbia Sportswear reports worldwide sales of $350 million in 1997, up from $299 million in 1996. Founded in 1938 in Portland, Oregon, Columbia Sportswear Company is the world's largest skiwear manufacturer. Its active outdoor apparel and footwear is sold through more than 10,000 retailers worldwide.

Source: Columbia Sportswear Company press release, www.columbia.com/columbia/company/release3.htm, accessed May 29, 1998.

FIGURE 7.2   <u>DISTINCTIVE COMPETENCY IDENTIFICATION PROCESS</u>

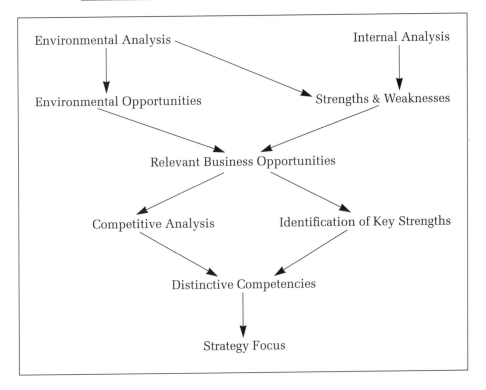

ties most consistent with a firm's competencies are the ones that are actively pursued and become the focus for subsequent planning efforts.

A caveat: A business may succeed without a specific distinctive competence. In particular, this may be true if consumer demand is strong in relation to industry supply; simply presenting the product or service to a ready market ensures at least short-term success. However, if business returns are attractive and no barriers impede new entrants into the industry, there will undoubtedly be an eventual competitive shakeout. It is then that the businesses with firmly established competencies have the greatest likelihood of survival.

COMPETITIVE WEAKNESSES

Although careful environmental and internal analyses enable managers to identify areas of distinctive competence, they also suggest areas of competitive weakness—that is, an area of vulnerability in which competitors have a meaningful edge. In a highly competitive situation, one firm's distinctive competency is often another firm's competitive weakness. Just as distinctive competencies are developed over time, competitive weaknesses, too, typically evolve over time.

Throughout its business life, actions a company has taken or failed to take can accrue into competitive weaknesses. Once recognized, however, competitive weaknesses can motivate the strategy process. Managers should respond in order to minimize, mitigate, or overcome areas of distinctive weakness.

Consider the following example of how a business can respond to a competitive weakness and build a strategy for competitive success. Alan Wolan started Five Fingers Inc. in 1995 on an investment of only $15,000. His concept was basic but timely—sell advertising on free postcards, an idea so popular in the trendy bars, restaurants, and health clubs in New York City that revenues reached $25,000 a month by the end of the first year. As he considered expanding, Wolan found other entrepreneurs had tapped the same niche in other big cities, posing a threat he hadn't expected. Even more bothersome, a large competitor, Max Racks, was ready to invade major metro areas. Confronted with impending and crippling competition, Wolan faced the reality of a true competitive weakness. While Wolan lacked the money to expand his business, his new rival—Max Racks—had deep coffers. Viewing Max as the common enemy, Wolan "partnered" with similar businesses in Los Angeles and Chicago. Their new business, GoCard Postcard Advertising, became a network that soon expanded to include seven small companies in 14 cities. They were able to expand quickly, attract clients nationwide, and fend off a bigger competitor.[3] A competitive weakness had spawned a creative and winning strategic response.

THE CONSULTANT'S VIEWPOINT

Types of Distinctive Competence

Distinctive competencies can take the form of either resources, something the firm has, or capabilities, something the firm does. Consultants must not only stress the need to develop distinctive competencies but also the need to develop complementary sources of distinctive competencies. If a client can develop a resource as a distinctive competence, let's say a superior product, then the client must develop capabilities (e.g., processes) that support the product. If a client can't develop both types of distinctive competencies—resources and capabilities—not only will this limit the firm's exploitative opportunities, but it may also make it easy for competitors to imitate the competencies.

Consider EMI, Ltd., the company that introduced the CAT scanner, a machine used by the medical profession to, among other things, detect cancer. (In fact, the EMI research engineer who invented the machine won a Nobel prize for doing so.) Initially, EMI was the only company that knew how to make CAT scanners, and thus it clearly possessed a tangible resource (technology) as a source of distinctive competence. Unfortunately, however, it did not have the capabilities (service and support staff) to exploit its resource. General Electric, with its sophisticated manufacturing processes and a sizable sales force, saw the opportunity for CAT scanner sales. GE manufactured a modified version of EMI's invention (to work around the patent) and eventually benefited most from the machine.[4]

Difficulties in Assessing Competitive Weaknesses

Managers of emerging companies are often enamored of their products and businesses but may have great difficulty in recognizing competitive weaknesses. This difficulty generally stems both from an unrealistic analysis of the competitive environment and from an inadequate internal analysis. This is why it is so important that consultants stress a sound and objective analysis and why managers must be open and ready to accept and respond to the outcomes of the analysis. As an outsider to the firm, a consultant may identify competitive weaknesses much easier than an insider, but the identification must be performed diplomatically to avoid damaging a client's ego. A consultant should be as objective as possible, citing factual information rather than relying on opinions. In addition, when identifying competitive weaknesses, a consultant should focus on being constructive. Rather than discussing why the firm has a specific weakness, the focus should be on strategies to minimize and eventually eliminate the weakness.

Indeed, one or two key areas of competitive weaknesses can, if unrealized and unattended, destroy the base of strength derived from a series of distinctive competencies. Because few businesses are best at everything, a consultant can stress that having a competitive weakness is not a sign of failure. Instead, it signals that there are factors for a company to deal with in its development of goals and strategy for competitive action.

DISCUSSION QUESTIONS

1. How can distinctive competencies be identified?
2. Can distinctive competencies really be developed as part of a strategy or are they simply something a firm has or doesn't have?
3. How necessary is it for a firm to develop a particular distinctive competence?
4. Pick a company that you know something about. Does it have distinctive competencies? How does or should the firm exploit them?
5. What kinds of competencies might we expect in the following businesses?
   a. a shoe store
   b. a grocery store
   c. a pet shop
   d. a heating and air-conditioning firm
   e. a computer repair business

NOTES

1. For a more in-depth discussion of competencies and their sources, see Arthur A. Thompson, Jr., and A. J. Strickland III, *Strategic Management: Concepts and Cases,* 10th ed. (Burr Ridge, Illinois: Irwin McGraw-Hill, 1998), Chapter 4.

2. Alessandra Bianchi, "DNA-Like Toy Inspires Brand Creation," *Inc.,* March, 1998, pp. 21–22.

3. Mike Hoffman, "Dear Max: Drop Dead. Love, GoCard," *Inc.,* April, 1997, p. 28.

4. Charles W. L. Hill and Gareth R. Jones, *Strategic Management: An Integrated Approach,* 4th ed. (Boston: Houghton Mifflin, 1998), pp. 217, 220.

GROWTH STRATEGIES FOR NEW AND EMERGING BUSINESSES

We turn now to the action phase of the strategic planning process in which the actual strategic plan is developed. Growth strategies set the tone for a business and become the focus for unit-level goals and strategies. The particular growth strategies that are implemented will depend on the strengths and weaknesses of the firm and the nature of the firm's environment. After reading this chapter, you should be able to

- differentiate types of growth strategies common to emerging businesses;
- comprehend how a company's vision and mission, external and internal analyses, and distinctive competencies all impact its strategies;
- understand how strategic alliances can assist an emerging business pursue growth; and
- recognize the factors to be considered when choosing a growth strategy.

A growth strategy should reflect how a business will behave in attempting to achieve its overall mission and secure a competitive advantage. It is management's approach for positioning the business in response to external opportunities and threats, internal strengths and weaknesses, and distinctive competencies the business has developed.

Small businesses often fail to develop an overall growth strategy and instead emphasize short-term goals and operational decisions. In such cases, a firm's strategic orientation evolves as a reflection of past actions—it describes what a firm has done rather than prescribing what the business will do—and fails to reinforce a sense of future direction. We recommend that managers of emerging businesses take time to formally consider the overall company strategies they desire.

Growth strategies enable managers to lead their business toward its vision and mission. Growth strategies can focus on markets, products, or a combination of the two. Figure 8.1 illustrates how the pursuit of markets and products yields different growth strategies.

New and emerging businesses can realize growth by creating a competitive advantage in a specific product and market segment using a focus strategy. They can also pursue growth opportunities by developing

FIGURE 8.1   TOPOLOGY OF GROWTH STRATEGIES

	Market	
	Existing	New
Existing	Focus Strategies •Product niche •Market niche	Market Development Strategies •Internal development •Franchising •Strategic alliance
Product		
New	Product Development Strategies •Incremental •Radical	Diversification Strategies •Related •Unrelated

new markets for existing products using a market development strategy or developing new products for existing markets using a product development strategy. Finally, emerging businesses can pursue growth by developing new products for new markets using a diversification strategy.

FOCUS STRATEGIES

New and emerging companies can pursue growth by creating a competitive advantage in an existing market with an existing product, an approach typically referred to as a focus strategy and the most prevalent strategy used by smaller businesses. The appeal of pursuing growth through a focus strategy is a company's ability to exploit a single competitive advantage, thus allowing a small business to emphasize what it knows and does best. Small-business success—at least initially—is enhanced by limiting involvement to those areas in which owners and managers have relevant business experience and an understanding of the dynamics of the competitive market situation. This is especially true when the managerial staff is limited. Focusing on a single product and market niche allows busy managers to concentrate on the nuances of that particular situation. Managers can orient and target their energies in a unique and focused direction and thereby improve their chances of staying on top of relevant issues and competitive factors—the primary reason why new businesses are often well advised to begin with a focus strategy.

An example of a focus strategy in an emerging business is seen in Kurzweil Educational Systems, a company started by Ray Kurzweil in 1996. After owning a number of other companies, Kurzweil launched a company that sells educational software for blind students and students with learning disabilities. Kurzweil Educational Systems, Inc. (KESI), developed the Kurzweil 1000 for people who are blind or visually impaired and the Kurzweil 3000 for people with learning disabilities and reading difficulties. Both products work by scanning virtually any printed document into a PC and converting the text into speech. The Kurzweil 3000 presents readers with a true-to-life, full-color image of an entire page, including photos, graphics, and captions. The software then reads each word aloud in a realistic-sounding synthesized voice, and each word or phrase is highlighted on the screen as it's being spoken, making it easy to follow printed material and reinforcing reading skills and comprehension.

The company focuses on a single market: students with disabilities. And it focuses on a single product line: educational software that converts text to speech. Because 15 million people in the United States have some type of learning disability the growth potential of Kurzweil's market is quite attractive.[1]

By using a focus strategy, a smaller business can develop a number of potential competitive advantages over larger firms. Small businesses are typically characterized by flexibility and adaptability, factors that enable a new or emerging firm to meet the special needs of its target market in a more timely and responsive manner than can a larger business. A smaller business can exploit opportunities that are normally overlooked or bypassed by larger firms. Profile 8.1 is an example of how a company has used a focus strategy to achieve growth.

Of course, implementing a focus strategy can be risky. If the present product or market remains dynamic, the strategy can lead to significant growth, but if either the product or the market loses its vitality, the business is on tenuous ground and may need to be repositioned. The essence of this orientation can be found in Mark Twain's caveat, "Put all your eggs in one basket and guard the basket."

MARKET DEVELOPMENT STRATEGIES

Market development strategies can be an effective way to achieve growth by extending existing products into new markets. These strategies can be of two types. The first is geographical expansion whereby the product remains unchanged. The business continues to emphasize the customer and product characteristics that have provided past success, but new geographical markets for existing product lines are identified and tapped. This is a common way for emerging businesses to implement growth. In retail, for example, as one unit becomes successful, additional stores are opened in other suburbs or cities.

The second method of market development is selling the same or similar products to new target markets. An example of this latter case is a local Edward Jones financial services office. In reviewing current customer lists, the owner noted a predominance of men. Realizing a wide base of professional women existed that most financial service businesses had not effectively captured, the owner decided to offer the same basic services targeted

PROFILE 8.1

The Blue Ribbon Car Wash

Sue and Jim Acres operate the Blue Ribbon Car Wash in a growing and affluent part of a medium-sized city. They don't market the car wash to the general public nor would the general public typically frequent it. Charging more than $40 per wash ($60 for a wash and wax), Blue Ribbon caters only to those who drive an expensive car like a Mercedes, BMW, Audi, Cadillac, Lexus, or Lincoln. Cars are accepted by appointment only and must be left for at least four hours. The cars are washed and polished by hand using only top-quality cleaners and waxes. They are cleaned and vacuumed inside, and fabric protector is applied if the owner wants. Wheels are scrubbed and wire wheels are carefully attended to—with a toothbrush if necessary. For an additional charge, the engine compartment will be cleaned, the trunk vacuumed, and the oil changed. Sue reports that initially business was slow. However, by focusing on a specific market segment with a unique service, Sue projects business will triple over the next two years. She is even considering whether they will have to extend their hours and hire more people to meet rising demand.

to women. In fact, she periodically offers free investment seminars aimed specifically at women. Of course, investing by women is little different from investing by men. In this case, therefore, the product or service was essentially the same but the target market was different.

One of the key advantages of a market development strategy is that the business maintains a high degree of consistency and stability. For example, after a business has used a focus strategy successfully, the manager realizes additional markets can be captured using the same products or services. In this case, the business adopts a market development strategy that has evolved from the successful implementation of a focus strategy. Because of past success and a promising outlook, managers come to recognize the opportunities in geographically expanding the company's market or expanding to a new target market. An emerging business can pursue a market development strategy through (1) internal development, (2) franchising, or (3) strategic alliances.

Internal Development

Internal development is an approach to implementing a market development strategy in which a business enters new markets on its own. The manager of an emerging business identifies a new location; provides any necessary capital, equipment, and human resources; and manages any new facilities. This approach has three major advantages. First, the manager has complete control over how new locations operate. This can become an important issue, especially if a source of distinctive competence comes from the way in which a business is managed. Second, all profits are kept by the business rather than sharing them with partners. Third, the company may realize economies of scale that occur when a firm can lower its average cost of operations by increasing the size of its production or service facilities and its production volume.

While there are considerable advantages to expanding markets through internal development, there are also two major disadvantages. First, market development via internal development can be very expensive; many small firms may not have the money to finance such an approach to expanding into new markets. The second major disadvantage is that the small firm may not understand the nuances of markets in which it wants to locate, such as brand loyalty to existing locally owned businesses.

Crystal Rug Cleaners is a good example of a company that successfully pursued a market development strategy using the internal development approach after it had successfully used a focus strategy. An overview of Crystal is presented in Profile 8.2.

Crystal's basic strengths of service, professionalism, and knowledge of proper cleaning procedures were maintained and stressed in advertising messages geared to the new market segment. Making such a strategic change requires care. The business must be sure that in addressing new markets, the needs of the established markets are not forgotten or confused. Implementing a market development strategy through internal development does add planning complexity but remains a logical means of fostering continued growth.

PROFILE 8.2

Crystal Rug Cleaners

Crystal Rug Cleaners was started in an exclusive section of Florida's Gulf Coast in the early 1990s by Michael Richards. Initially, Richards's environmental assessment revealed a promising opportunity. First, the market boasted extremely high levels of income. Homes were large and expensive, and quality carpeting and rugs were common. Although there were a number of cleaning firms in the area, none had established themselves as quality businesses specializing in carpeting. The upper-income market was reluctant to entrust its cleaning needs to most of the operations already doing business, particularly because incorrect cleaning methods can damage or ruin expensive carpets. Richards trained extensively in cleaning methods and techniques, including those unique to high-grade and Oriental carpets, and Crystal Rug Cleaners was licensed by the National Institute of Rug Cleaners, the first and only cleaner in the market area to earn such a distinction. To highlight his competence and expertise, Richards limited his firm's activities to carpet and rug cleaning. By distinguishing himself from his competitors and focusing on a single product/market orientation, Richards made his business prosper and grow.

Within three years, he had saturated his current market, thus diminishing the opportunity for additional growth. Using excess profits, Richards decided to establish satellite operations in nearby communities that offered the same services he had so successfully provided before. The expansion did not occur piecemeal but was carefully planned. Richards made supportable projections of increased demand for each new market and budgeted his costs and returns accordingly.

Franchising

If a company doesn't have the resources to pursue market development on its own, or if the manager desires rapid expansion, franchising may be considered. Franchising occurs when a business—the franchiser—grants exclusive rights to another individual or business—the franchisee—to use its name or services. Becoming a franchiser has several advantages. First, fewer resources are required to develop markets, although the costs to initially set up a franchising system can be quite high. Second, because markets can be developed faster, economies of scale can be achieved in areas such as advertising, distribution, and product development. Third, selling franchises to franchisees creates highly motivated owners of individual franchises, who often invest considerable funds and time to make their franchise work. Further, the added number of units creates both visibility and respectability as customers see the units on more and more street corners. The major disadvantage to the franchiser is reduced profits and loss of control. For a company whose distinctive competence is quality, such as Crystal Rug Cleaners, franchising has to be pursued with great care to ensure that quality is being maintained.

Strategic Alliances

Many times a manager who wants to aggressively pursue market development realizes, after assessing the firm's relative competitive strengths, that the firm doesn't have the necessary resources or capabilities. In these instances, rather than forgoing pursuit of a market opportunity, the manager may consider forming a strategic alliance with one or more other firms. Two or more businesses in strategic alliances share resources or capabilities in areas where each is distinctly qualified. This can be an effective growth strategy when those in the alliance contribute in their own areas of strength; businesses choose to work with each other in fact when their strengths complement each other. A strategic alliance allows partners to share costs and move forward in a highly efficient manner, but it works only when each partner brings valued strengths to the alliance and can trust other participants to do their part.

Strategic alliances are particularly effective growth strategies for new and emerging businesses when they possess distinctive competencies but don't have the ability to exploit them. The strategic alliance can provide this ability and thus build a true competitive advantage.

Although strategic alliances can be used in focus strategies and in product development strategies, their most frequent and logical use in emerging businesses is for moving from an existing market into new markets. The benefit of strategic alliances can be seen in Profile 8.3.

PROFILE 8.3

ModaCAD, Inc.

ModaCAD, Inc., is a small software developer with a potentially valuable distinctive competence. The company spent several years developing Project New York, a virtual mall on the Internet where shoppers can walk and visit stores whose layout and decor are almost identical to those of the actual stores. The program produces 3D images of clothing and other products that shoppers can purchase through their home computer. Shoppers can click on a rack of clothes, try something on a mannequin, and even click on an accompanying article of clothing from another store to create a whole outfit.

After focus groups told ModaCAD it would be fun to take friends along when shopping, ModaCAD now lets two users visit a store at the same time, shop for clothes, and make comments in a chat area on the computer screen.

Although ModaCAD had a distinctive resource competence, it also had two problems: (1) it didn't have the capability to mass market its product, and (2) the program required hundreds of thousands of coding lines to be loaded onto the user's home computer. How would ModaCAD convince consumers to load such a large program on their home computers to shop the virtual mall?

Because ModaCAD didn't have the capability to exploit its distinctive competence, its management decided to pursue a strategic alliance with Intel Corporation to provide the missing resources needed to make Project New York a success. Intel has convinced many computer manufacturers to produce its machines with the ModaCAD software already loaded. In addition, ModaCAD's software has been carefully developed for use on a new generation of Intel chips that haven't yet reached the market. Clearly, ModaCAD has used a strategic alliance to pursue growth opportunities that would have been extremely difficult—if not impossible—to pursue on its own.

Source: Frederick Rose, "ModaCAD Aims to Bridge Real Gaps in Virtual Mall," *The Wall Street Journal,* May 14, 1998, p. B6.

PRODUCT DEVELOPMENT STRATEGIES

In contrast to market development, product development strategies stress variations or improvements in a firm's products, which are introduced to existing markets. Managers hope that the positive image customers have of existing products will carry over to the new products. This growth strategy can be pursued through either incremental or radical product development.

With incremental product development, a firm makes modifications to existing products in current markets. Present customers (with assumed loyalty) are maintained and targeted while product variations are introduced. Incremental product development involves product variations and improvements but no overriding change in the fundamental product.

Radical product development, on the other hand, seeks so novel an alteration of the existing product that a totally new or different product is created. With radical product development, existing products are not eliminated; growth comes from sales of both the derivative product and the existing one. The same customers may buy both the existing products and the new products.

Although product development is generally assumed to be a feature of larger firms with well-supported research and development staffs, many contemporary product advances have come from emerging entrepreneurial companies. Advances in microcomputer hardware and software are common examples. Emerging businesses—working intensively and hands-on with a particular product every day—often generate meaningful product innovations.

A product development strategy may be adopted by service companies as well as by manufacturers. For example, Copper's Cabinetry operated for four years as a fledgling operation that specialized in building and renovating closets in customers' homes. Today, operating as Copper's Consultants, it advises harried, time-conscious clients how to organize their life to eliminate daily time wasters. The service includes everything from redesigning and rearranging wardrobe closets with customized modifications to adding mirrors to shower stalls so that shaving and brushing teeth can be done while showering. Consumers are willing to pay for the added control they gain over their time and routines. The company's business is steadily increasing among dual-income, upper-middle-class households.

One reason product development is so attractive is the possibility it offers for high returns. Introducing new services or products can bring big profits—at least until competitors recognize and respond to the changes. But significant risks are also present. Being on the cutting edge demands a careful and accurate reading of environmental trends as well as a timely and cost-effective response.

DIVERSIFICATION STRATEGIES

Because a company pursuing a diversification strategy will enter new markets with new products, diversification strategies encompass both market and product development. Although a core area of concentration may still command the bulk of the business's energies, the business is extending into other products, markets, or services.

A business may move to a diversification strategy for a number of reasons, but an emerging business typically diversifies for growth-related reasons. In other words, managers realize that excellent opportunities for continued and expanded growth exist by moving into additional areas of business.

Related Diversification

Diversification can be of two types: related or unrelated. In related diversification, the new business has some tie to the existing business. Strategists refer to this tie as strategic fit. Strategic fit can be product related or process related. If the new business is product related, it may be within the same general industry as existing products while still being substantially different. For example, a software development company that makes educational software may decide to create financial software. Here the strategic fit is software development products even though the specific market and the nature of the products are quite different. In process-related diversification, the strategic fit is an internal process, skill, or competence that can be transferred to the new business. For example, a growing business that produces plastic fittings for industrial products realizes that the process of forming the fittings is equally applicable in such consumer products as garden hose connectors. Accordingly, it extends its business into an entirely new area, offering a new product directed to a totally different market—a full-line garden equipment manufacturer. In both product-related and process-related diversification, there is a key logic or strategic fit between existing and new business ventures.

Many experts suggest that emerging businesses, because of their size, are wise to expand where there is some logical relationship—a strategic fit—between existing operations and desired areas of diversification. A business is at extremely high risk when its expansion extends beyond its realm of experience or demonstrated competence.

Again, Crystal Rug Cleaners is a meaningful example. Crystal grew and prospered by selecting meaningful niches and selected growth strategies. When Richards realized that Crystal's level of professionalism and quality would prompt consumers to trust Crystal with other carpeting services, he considered diversification. Given the company's quality reputation, Richards decided to expand into full-line commercial cleaning services. This meant that new markets had to be tapped and new skills developed. Additional employees were hired and special equipment and supplies were purchased. Within a year, commercial cleaning services, a logical area of complementary growth, were contributing nearly as much revenue as the original carpet cleaning business.

Unrelated Diversification

Although unrelated diversification may be less common and riskier for an emerging business, it is, nonetheless, a strategic option. At times, opportunities arise that are appealing even though totally unrelated to the existing business. Often, such unrelated diversification is more spontaneous than related diversification, but unrelated diversification may be a well thought out and conscious strategy to avoid putting all one's eggs in a single basket. The owner of a successful and growing insurance business, for example, realized that his growing cash flow could underwrite one or more additional ventures. As a hedge against the volatility and threatened regulatory emphasis of the insurance industry, he decided to invest in a multiunit restaurant franchise.

Diversification can be extremely beneficial either when the existing product or service is risky or when dark clouds are gathering over the product. Diversification has the potential of offsetting possible downturns in other products. Regardless of whether diversification is related or unrelated, it is a strategy that can yield high returns if done well.

SELECTING AN APPROPRIATE GROWTH STRATEGY

Given the four general growth strategies available to emerging businesses, managers must decide which are the most appropriate for their particular situation. Clear, obvious answers are rare, and exceptions are common. However, two factors may help to determine when each strategy is most appropriate—the growth potential of the company's industry and the firm's relative competitive strengths. Industry growth potential must be assessed not only in the present but projected over the firm's planning horizon. A careful and thorough environmental analysis should provide enough information to decide if industry growth potential is relatively strong or relatively weak. Much of the material in Chapters 3 and 4 applies here. Managers should consider the interplay of industry growth and competitive strengths when selecting a strategy.

High-Growth Industry Situations

The most appropriate strategic decision for an emerging firm in an industry that has high growth potential is to continue with a focus strategy. In this case, rather than considering expansion into new areas, managers should invest resources into its existing industry to achieve future growth. Because many emerging companies have limited resources, investment in a different industry would take resources away from a firm's current industry—an industry that has already exhibited growth and in which the firm has already gained expertise.

A market development or product development strategy may be effective under high-growth conditions, but a business must be careful before embracing either of these strategies. Generally, an emerging business would only consider product or market development if it has distinctive competencies that can be readily applied to new products or markets.

In cases where a firm faces a high-growth market but doesn't have sufficient resources to capture that market alone, franchising or strategic alliances can resolve the dilemma; the firm achieves growth by partnering with other firms. Partnering through franchising allows the business to be replicated over and over with franchisees, and a strategic alliance with another firm provides assistance in the manufacture and/or distribution of the product.

Firms following a focus or strategic alliance strategy typically have competitive strengths or distinctive competencies. A firm in a high-growth industry, however, may still achieve significant growth without any competitive strengths. Demand may be so strong that any firm able to deliver the desired product to customers will succeed. Because such a rosy condition is always temporal, care must be exercised here. Eventually, industry growth will begin to stabilize and subside, and those businesses without competitive strengths and distinctive competencies will be most vulnerable. Accordingly, emphasizing company strengths during times of growth can be a prudent and proactive measure.

Lower-Growth Industry Situations

Market development and product development strategies become more relevant when a manager's analysis of the industry environment suggests that growth may be or soon will be tapering off. Then the firm capitalizes on one or more of its competitive strengths to expand and grow. Expansion may be through the development of new products to sell to existing target markets—product development. Or the firm may find ways to sell existing products to new target markets—market development. In either case, the firm's sales should increase in spite of slowing industry growth.

If industry growth is clearly on the wane, diversification must be considered. The manager must reconsider the environment and assess whether the company has competitive strengths that could be applied in new industries. Realistically, diversification is probably the least likely strategy for emerging firms and is certainly one of the riskiest strategies a business could adopt, although significant company strengths, in terms of processes or products, can often be the key to related diversification efforts. In such cases, the manager redirects the firm's efforts to new products and target markets while keeping some tie to the current operation.

Unrelated diversification may be considered in some rare circumstances when the manager determines that completely different challenges should be considered. The unrelated diversification may be a defensive move when the manager feels that the current industry is threatened, or it can be an offensive move when the manager realizes that excess funds need to be invested outside the current industry. The latter case may arise when government regulation threatens an industry or when demographics or other social changes signal severe problems in the future.

THE CONSULTANT'S VIEWPOINT

In developing a strategic plan and recommending appropriate growth strategies, the consultant must assess future growth potential and growth-related opportunities. Remember that growth potential is a function of environmental factors, internal strengths and weaknesses, and managers' attitudes. After carefully examining these considerations, the consultant may wish to proceed with a plan or reevaluate growth projections.

The consultant must also help the client recognize the importance of controlled growth. Many small businesses want to pursue growth. Growth is exciting, challenging, and may provide managers with a sense of prestige, but these are the wrong reasons for such a pursuit. Rather than pursuing growth simply for excitement or enhancing egos, managers of emerging businesses should have a rational purpose, such as improving the company's long-term competitive position, for engaging in the pursuit of growth.

Companies that experience growth usually have to make several sacrifices. One short-term sacrifice may be profit. Many emerging businesses have impressive revenue growth. Profitability, however, may be at the same level or even lower than it was before growth began. When a firm commits to a growth-based orientation, resources have to be committed to product and/or market development so that in the short run, growth may not lead to profitability.

In addition, growth has some serious risks. Success may put a company out of business if it grows too fast. Examples abound of companies that have been forced to close their doors because they grew too fast. Let's assume a small retailer had a competitive advantage in a reputation for service. As the company grew in size, its service eroded because employees were too busy trying to keep up with demand rather than providing excellent service. The reputation that made the company successful is now the reason the company is out of business.

Given the potential risks, why do so many firms still desire growth? If planned correctly, growth can provide benefits by increasing the company's competitive position, power base, survivability, cost position, and long-term profitability.

A consultant can help to guide a company to achieve beneficial growth rather than detrimental growth by stressing balance. Proper planning for growth requires focus not only on growth goals but also on operational goals. The consultant should emphasize that the firm needs to achieve *controlled* growth. Rather than increasing in size as fast as possible and worrying about how to manage the growth at a later date, the consultant needs to emphasize balance between resources allocated for growth and resources allocated for effectively managing growth.

DISCUSSION QUESTIONS

1. Is it necessary to have a strategic approach to growth? Why or why not?
2. Explain when one growth strategy would be preferable to another.
3. Select the growth strategy most appropriate for each of the following:
   a. a new computer chip manufacturer
   b. a real estate firm dealing with commercial property
   c. an older grocery store located in a growing community
5. What are some of the advantages and disadvantages of forming a strategic alliance?

NOTES

1. www.kurzweiledu.com, accessed November 9, 1998.

CHAPTER 9

SETTING GOALS

A company's first action step—defining its strategies for growth—is based on an analysis of the firm's capabilities and its environment. Yet simply determining broad strategies is insufficient. Those strategies must be converted into goals for the business as a whole and for the units within the business. The goals then serve as the basis for more specific strategies and tactics. Determining specific goals for a business is the focus of this chapter. (The differences between goals and objectives here are negligible, so we use the terms interchangeably.) After studying the chapter, you should be able to

- describe the relationship between goals on the one hand and the vision, mission, and growth strategy of the business on the other;
- visualize the process of determining goals;
- differentiate between horizon goals and near-term goals;
- understand the difference between companywide goals and unit goals; and
- segment goals into action plans.

BENEFITS OF SPECIFIC GOALS

Suppose you and a friend are leisurely driving around the city some Sunday afternoon, and you realize that you have no idea where you are. Are you lost? The answer is no. But suppose one of you suddenly says, "It's four o'clock! We were supposed to be at a meeting fifteen minutes ago!" Now you are lost.

The leisurely Sunday afternoon drive was fine as long as the only goal was to have a good time. But once you realized you had to be somewhere at a certain time (and you were late), you looked around for landmarks or asked directions. The point is that only if you have a specific goal to strive for do you take the actions necessary to achieve it.

This analogy speaks clearly to the business world. One of the fundamental dangers for new and emerging businesses is that they will simply "drive around," serving customers and working at a frenetic pace but lacking clarity of direction. Business goals provide the needed clarity and direction. Once a goal is set, performance can be measured in terms of that goal. Thus, a goal is simultaneously a planning tool and a control tool—a planning tool because it must precede the actual development of a plan and a control tool because it is a preset standard against which performance can be measured. If goals have not been achieved, corrective steps may be taken to improve performance.

Goals also motivate employees. Achievable goals, in fact, can become a rallying point for the entire company. Recently, the owner of a small manufacturing firm attributed her firm's ability to weather some tough economic and competitive times to the fact that the employees knew where the company was headed. They knew what the owners expected and had a good sense of what was likely to happen. She noted that sharing goals built a sense of identity and was convinced that the open sharing of goals fostered a "we are in this together" spirit that helped the firm rebound from some bleak days.

CHARACTERISTICS OF GOOD GOALS

If goals are to have meaning and the process of goal setting is to work, certain basic rules, guidelines, or considerations must be noted. In general, these rules apply to all types of goals.

First, goal statements should be phrased in terms of outcomes or results rather than processes. Managers must focus on desired accomplishments, not the series of activities undertaken to achieve these accomplishments. There is a world of difference between saying, "This week we will work on the budget," and "By the end of this week, the budget will be completed."

Second, goal statements should be clear, specific, and, to the extent possible, quantifiable or measurable. The clearer and more precise the goal, the greater the likelihood that it will be pursued and attained. It is simplistic to say that you cannot control what you do not measure. Yet if managers want high levels of performance from workers, the workers have to understand precisely what end result is expected. General platitudes are not acceptable. In fact, to be most useful, goals should be cast in terms of percentage increases from a baseline. Thus, a goal of a 5 percent increase in sales compared with last year is better than saying that we want to increase sales next month.

Third, effective goal statements should be challenging yet realistic. Challenging goals are essential for emerging businesses and growth-oriented owners. Goals that are too simple or too easily reached cheat the business of its full potential. They can lead employees to feel underutilized in their jobs and contribute to declines in morale and job satisfaction. On the other hand, goals that are too lofty may quickly be perceived as unreasonable or unrealistic, and employees will not even try to achieve them.

Finally, goals must be communicated throughout the organization. Regardless of how impressive a goal statement may be in meeting the foregoing criteria, its potential to influence behavior is lost if it is not communicated to employees. Many managers understand the value of open communication and include their employees in the goal-setting process, which not only enhances the goals but becomes a key to motivation. The empowerment movement of recent years focuses on mutual understanding, involvement, and agreement between owners and employees about goal setting.

To summarize, goals should be

- phrased in terms of outcomes rather than actions;
- measurable;
- challenging yet realistic; and
- communicated.

HOW ARE GOALS CREATED?

Although setting viable goals is largely a judgmental process, it should not be done by the seat of the pants. In part, goal setting should be based on historical data, but to a greater extent it should be based on the analyses discussed in Chapters 4, 5, and 6.

The focus of goals may change from time to time. Suppose, for example, that sales have increased as planned over the past several years, but costs have risen dramatically. The goal for the next period may focus on cost containment. Sales increases may still be encouraged, but the primary emphasis will be on reducing expenses per sales dollar.

Often, a specific numerical goal will be a compromise among key management personnel. The marketing manager may suggest a target increase in sales of, say, 10 percent. The controller may be more pessimistic and feel that 6 percent is the most that could be expected. The production manager may be pretty sure that 7 or 8 percent is the maximum increase obtainable without a substantial capital outlay. The owner, working with these managers, encourages each person to offer a sales forecast for the coming year along with related information, and together they set final goals for the year. Open communication becomes a key to meaningful compromise.

Conflict among Goals

No business will have a single overriding goal. All groups, all businesses, all individuals have multiple goals. Many of the goals are congruous, but some will be in conflict. For example, a goal to be a successful business owner sometimes conflicts with a goal to be a successful parent.

Managers of a business may even have mutually exclusive goals. One manager may have a goal in conflict with another manager, or a manager may have two goals that conflict with each other. In either case the exclusivity means that one cannot be achieved without serious damage to the other. For both new and emerging businesses, conflict among goals can affect the strategy of the firm. One group of managers, for example, may want to commit funds to introduce the firm's products into new markets. Another group may be convinced that funds need to be allocated to technological improvements and product modifications to keep up with changes in the industry. Both groups argue that their goal is the best way for the business to achieve growth. Because of limited funds, both sets of goals cannot be pursued so the conflicts must be resolved or internal dissension and indecision can cripple the business.

Goal Priorities

Everyone establishes priorities because people can never attain all that they want to attain or do all that they want to do. Thus, people learn to prioritize and determine which of life's objectives are most important. Businesses too have multiple opportunities and multiple goals, and it is difficult, if not impossible, to achieve all of them. This is particularly true for the emerging business where growth may present an array of opportunities, making it necessary, then, for the company to set priorities for its goals. Owners may decide that the major emphasis this year will be on hiring new employees because the major emphasis last year was on expanding into a new area. Sales may have increased dramatically, but now personnel needs must be addressed. Although growth and expansion received top priority last year, they now must take second place to human resource considerations.

Setting priorities for goals is particularly important in product development. If a firm has a number of products that could be marketed, it may decide that products A and B will receive attention and funding next year and products C, D, and E the following year. Similarly, the firm may budget to replace some old equipment this year and schedule the remainder for replacement two years from now.

LEVELS AND TIME FRAMES

Goal setting is often seen as a complex process, and owners of small firms bristle at the thought of wading through the necessary procedures. This is unfortunate because goal setting need not be overly cumbersome.

All goals are not the same; there are different levels and types. While such distinctions may appear to complicate the goal-setting process, they are the basis for a logical system that allows the power of strategic goal setting to emerge.

Levels of Goals

As noted in Figure 9.1, two levels of goals—company and unit—are typical for new and emerging small businesses. Company goals relate to the performance or accomplishments of the overall business. Unit goals relate to the performance or accomplishments of one or more departments or units within the business. Figure 9.2 shows how company and unit goals differ yet relate to each other. A company goal establishes certain demands and requirements that need to be reflected in the unit goals.

For a manufacturing business to secure a 5 percent growth in revenues (company goal), for example, marketing must develop a more effective advertising and promotion scheme, operations must increase its capacity, the sales force must secure new contracts, and human resources must hire and train new workers. All these activities take place at the departmental level. Unit goals, then, help individual workers realize how their specialty fits into the overall business plan.

Unit goals must mesh with one another and with the overall business goals, but, unfortunately, contemporary business is plagued by the lack of integration of unit goals. For example, the marketing department may develop new promotional programs without much regard for how they affect other functional areas or the overall efficiency of the business. The marketing department may do an excellent job of securing new contracts or additional orders but, in the process, outsell the company's capacity to produce on time. Each unit must see itself as a part of the whole business. All must recognize that each part complements the other.

FIGURE 9.1

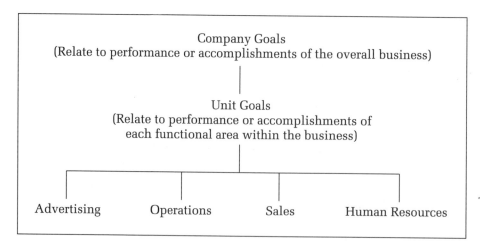

FIGURE 9.2

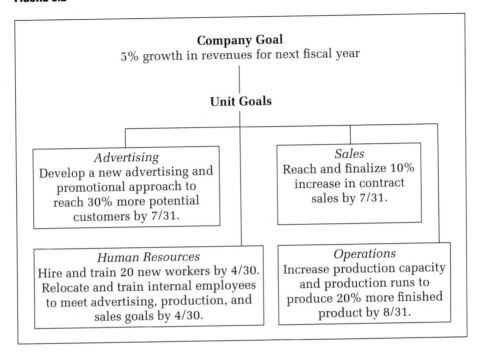

Company Goal
5% growth in revenues for next fiscal year

Unit Goals

Advertising
Develop a new advertising and promotional approach to reach 30% more potential customers by 7/31.

Sales
Reach and finalize 10% increase in contract sales by 7/31.

Human Resources
Hire and train 20 new workers by 4/30. Relocate and train internal employees to meet advertising, production, and sales goals by 4/30.

Operations
Increase production capacity and production runs to produce 20% more finished product by 8/31.

Company goals must precede unit goals. Company goals are established and then communicated to units. Unit managers then develop goals and review them with the owner to ensure that they fit properly with other unit goals and make an appropriate, balanced contribution to the business goals.

Goal Time Frames

New and emerging small businesses typically establish goals within three different time frames, as shown in Figure 9.3. These three time frames—horizon goals, near-term goals, and target goals—are interrelated and interdependent.

Horizon goals focus on accomplishments expected over the course of the firm's overall planning horizon. The longer-time nature of these goals means they involve relatively high levels of uncertainty. Horizon goals therefore tend to be broader and less specific than other types of goals.

Near-term goals are established to delineate results or accomplishments expected within the firm's next operating cycle. Although that

FIGURE 9.3   GOAL TIME FRAMES

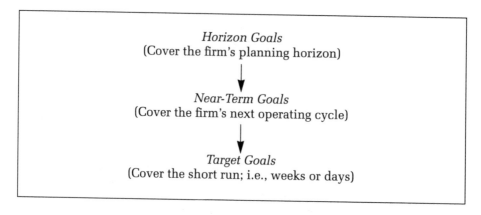

Horizon Goals
(Cover the firm's planning horizon)

Near-Term Goals
(Cover the firm's next operating cycle)

Target Goals
(Cover the short run; i.e., weeks or days)

period is industry and company specific, normally, near-term goals deal with the next six months to a year. Many companies, in fact, refer to these goals as short-term goals and assume that they are for one year.

From a planning perspective, horizon goals should be established before other goals. Often there is a strong temptation to think of the shorter-run, near-term goals as a starting point. If horizon goals are set first, however, the business must necessarily be analyzed with an eye on the distant future. Thus, horizon goals must reflect the company's vision (discussed in Chapter 3). All subsequent plans aim toward the longer-term goal rather than being unduly constrained with meeting near-term profitability or sales targets. At the very least, horizon goals should be developed for sales dollars, market share, dollar profits, cash flow, and return on investment.

Near-term goals are those portions of the horizon goals that can logically be obtained in a short period of time. For example, if the planning horizon for a manufacturing firm is five years and the horizon goal is to increase sales by 50 percent, then the near-term goal could logically be to increase sales by 10 percent over the next year. Similarly, a restaurant manager may have a three-year planning horizon and may want to have a new restaurant in place at the end of the three years. A near-term goal may be to accrue $100,000 in interest-bearing accessible funds by the middle of the current fiscal year while keeping the current ratio above 2.25. Near-term goals are the in-progress portion of horizon goals.

Once horizon and near-term goals have been determined, the final goal-setting task is to segment the near-term goals into target goals. Target goals refer to very short-term goals that are quite specific as to time and measurability. Target goals may generate actions that must be completed in a few weeks or even a few days.

Suppose a growing real estate business in Indianapolis has as one of its horizon goals to increase its market share for residential sales by 10 percent within five years. This goal may then be segmented into the near-term goal of increasing market share by 1 percent in year one, 2 percent in each of years two, three, and four, and 3 percent in year five. Target goals are then developed to refine the near-term goals into smaller, more workable units—increasing home sales by 10 percent in the first quarter, increasing listings by 20 percent, increasing sales per broker by 5 percent, and any other goal that will ultimately lead to the first-year 1 percent increase in market share. Finally, specific actions are developed to achieve those target goals.

The key to target goals is to make them very specific, measurable, and attainable. Once all the target goals are defined, they must then be checked to ensure that they mesh with the larger or longer near-term goals. Some target goals will change monthly, some will change weekly, and very specific targets might change daily. Although target goals should be included in the strategic plan, they should be physically easy to remove (included in an appendix, for example), because the targets may change frequently. But it is still necessary to write down the target goals and their related activities in order to communicate them, get commitment, and help direct employees.

THE GOAL SEGMENTATION PROCESS

The process of strategic goal setting is the same for company-level and unit-level goals. In fact, there should be horizon and near-term goals for both company and unit levels (see Figure 9.4). Target goals are generally developed for the units of the company.

Unfortunately, many small business owners develop goal statements that are so broad and ambiguous that they are merely platitudes. These dream-list approaches do little to provide a clear focus and direction for business activity or to offer meaningful indicators of business progress or necessary corrective actions. Moving incrementally from horizon to target goals forces owners to work through this potential goal stalemate and to produce a series of relevant and significant target goals.

FIGURE 9.4

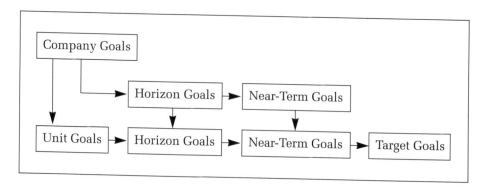

TARGET ACTION PLANS[1]

Once a set of horizon, near-term, and target goals has been developed and communicated, many owners of emerging firms think that planning has been accomplished, that further refinement is unnecessary. These managers will rarely see their goals reach fruition and will be understandably frustrated at having wasted so much time on the process. A target action plan, outlined in Figure 9.5, forces them to move beyond this scenario. It itemizes a series of tasks to be prescribed and accomplished in meeting each target goal. Figure 9.6 shows the target action plan for Uplands Supply, Inc., a growing manufacturer of ink cartridges used in copiers, fax machines, and printers. Uplands decided to use an advertising specialty campaign to promote its sales of ink cartridges to manufacturers of equipment that use the cartridges.

The first step in the target action plan is to restate the target goal in clear, precise, objective, results-oriented terms. In the Uplands example, the target goal is to develop an advertising specialty campaign within the next month, part of a larger near-term goal to increase sales by 15 percent over the next year. Even though the decision to use the advertising specialty approach had already been made, staff commitment to this approach has not been secured. With the target goal firmly in mind, a series of important action steps come into play, including determining any barriers that must be overcome, determining specific tasks that must be done, setting deadlines for completion, and identifying elements of feedback to use to assess results.

FIGURE 9.5

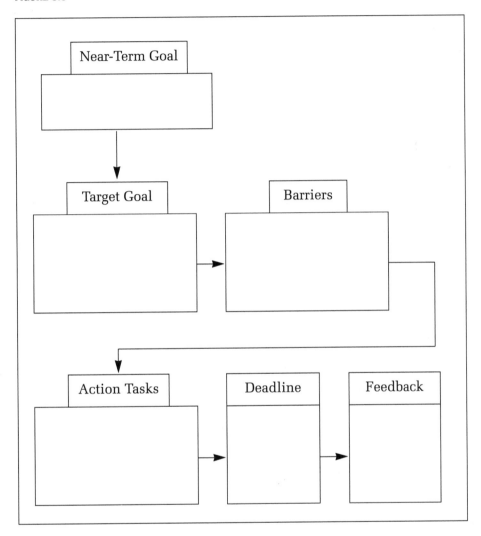

Barriers

Barriers are the obstacles or bottlenecks that must be overcome or cir-cumvented before target goals can be reached. It is critical that owners take the time to consider, in detail, the barriers that stand in the way of reaching target goals. Barriers typically relate to human resources, other resources, and time. The three types of barriers are (1) insurmountable

FIGURE 9.6

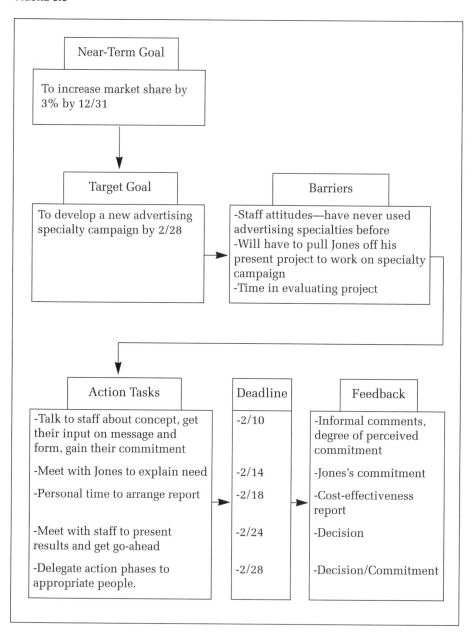

barriers, (2) barriers that can be overcome but only with a concerted redirection of effort toward the barrier, and (3) barriers that can be hurdled while enroute to the target goals.

The first type is a barrier or a series of barriers so overwhelming and significant that it is clear the target goal will never be attained. Suppose, for example, a company has a target goal of completing a marketing research project by the end of the month. If the two primary researchers on this project suddenly resign, the goal becomes unreachable. It is important to recognize an insurmountable goal early in the action process before you waste important resources and become frustrated. When you hit an insurmountable barrier, you need to abandon your target goal and consider alternatives.

The second type of barrier must be resolved before target goals can be addressed. This kind of barrier forces the owner to abandon the target goal temporarily and focus on overcoming the barrier. For example, if a machine is not performing to specifications, the target goal must be set aside and energies directed toward repairing the machine or acquiring a new one. Only then can the original target goal be addressed.

The third type of barrier is not as pervasive or overwhelming but still requires some sacrifice of resources or time. Owners must be aware of these sacrifices and be open and responsive to addressing these difficulties and explaining likely benefits if they are overcome. In the Uplands Supply example, the owners must convince the marketing department that time spent on advertising specialties is worthwhile and meaningful. They must also let the staff know what is expected of them, allaying their fears and apprehensions and encouraging a positive, supportive attitude.

Action Tasks

Action tasks are the specific tasks that must be completed if target goals are to be achieved. They are the final refinement in the process of segmenting goals into smaller, incremental units. These tasks, some of which may focus on dealing with barriers, are the most basic and narrowly defined. Each necessary action task must be noted. Once action tasks have been prescribed, they must be arranged into a logical sequence according to their priority. The specificity of the actions depends on the owner's confidence in employees. If employees are knowledgeable, dedicated, and innovative, action tasks are best stated in broad parameters, leaving it to the employees to determine specific activities. Conversely, if employees are new or unskilled, they may need more specificity and direction.

Deadlines

It is important to establish deadlines, or completion dates, for each task in the sequence. The deadlines must be real, not arbitrary, so employees treat them seriously. Imposing an artificially early deadline only frustrates employees, who no doubt have a number of simultaneous responsibilities. Deadlines should also be meaningful. Those for the most critical tasks—ones that if delayed will cause severe problems—should be set first. Deadlines for other tasks can then be assigned and arranged according to their priority.

Feedback

Some method of securing feedback should be determined in order to evaluate whether a task has been completed or is progressing as required. Feedback needs to give the owner a solid feel for the success of the task. Feedback regarding individual tasks may be easily identifiable, such as when an employee obtains a contract, or may be more qualitative, such as favorable comments from customers or an apparent increase in the ratio between sales calls and sales dollars. Monitoring feedback forces the owner to concentrate on action tasks and evaluate efforts to meet each part of the action task sequence. In the Uplands Supply, Inc., example, action tasks are listed in sequence according to their priority along with deadlines and a means of evaluative feedback for each.

The Integrative Goal Model

Thus far, we have identified four elements of strategic planning. First, the firm's mission and vision must be determined. Then, a broad situational analysis is performed, allowing the business to recognize its threats, opportunities, strengths, weaknesses, and relevant competencies. Companywide strategies must be developed, based on opportunities and threats, distinctive competencies, and the overall growth strategy chosen. In the next step, a series of goals is developed in the form of written, measurable goal statements. This series of goals clearly and specifically designates desired results. Finally, a target action plan is enacted to detail the process of bringing the goal statements to fruition. Figure 9.7 outlines this integrative goal model.

FIGURE 9.7

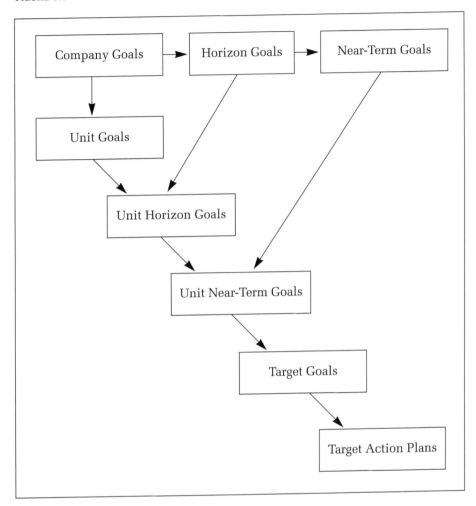

THE CONSULTANT'S VIEWPOINT

Goal setting is not an easy task. As many key people as possible should be brought into the goal-setting process even though the process can generate conflict among them. If one person sees that a redefined goal deemphasizes a preferred project, conflict can arise.

Consultants must not rush this process. A number of iterations may be necessary before finalized goals are reached. Communication is all-important. In working with clients, we occasionally suggest the mantra, "Communicate, communicate, communicate." Setting goals brings with it the need to consider changes in how the company operates to meet those goals, especially true in emerging companies. Because growth is occurring or is desired, managers must continually encourage employees to adapt to new strategies, new structures, and new goals despite perhaps a natural resistance. Thus, the goal-setting process must be handled carefully and with constant attention to the company's vision and mission.

We recommend focusing on the characteristics of good goals. Goals should be phrased in terms of outcomes rather than processes, they should be measurable, and they should be challenging yet realistic. By focusing on outcomes, getting bogged down in either processes or resource allocation can be avoided. As part of the communication process, it is necessary to instill in everyone's mind that it is the final result desired that drives everything else. If an intensive focus on goals and results can be developed, then the goals become the unifying force for the company. Once goals are agreed on, conflicts over resource allocation, company priorities, and strategies tend to subside. And once the mindset of key employees is clearly focused on goals and results, working to refine and segment goals both in terms of time lines and levels within the organization becomes clearer.

Employees should be encouraged to continually ask "what if" questions. The following examples are illustrative: "If we want the company to increase sales of Product A by 20 percent within three years, what should be our departmental or unit goals for the next year? For the next quarter?" "If we anticipate that our sales may double within two years (based on an analysis of the industry), what resources will we need to make that happen? How many employees will we need to hire? How many managers will we need? Do we have sufficient staff in the human resources department to accomplish that? Do we need to adjust our salary schedules in order to attract that many people?" "If we want to develop two new products per year in order to maintain the growth we envision, how much do we need to invest in research and development to ensure the accomplishment of the goal? Should we add more scientists or engineers in the R&D department, or can we gain more product development by restructuring into project teams?"

As seen from the above, the *process* of goal setting is often more important than the goals themselves because it encourages everyone to work together. We feel strongly that this unifying force is well worth the time it takes.

DISCUSSION QUESTIONS

1. How do a company's goals differ from its mission?
2. Historically, what is the relationship between goals and actual performance? Is the relationship different for an emerging firm compared with a slow-growing firm?
3. What process should be used to determine specific goals for an emerging business? Is this process different for a larger firm? For a not-for-profit organization?
4. What is the similarity between action tasks, as they relate to specific goals, and strategies, as they relate to broader goals?
5. How can specific functional areas have horizon-level goals?

NOTES

1. Many of the ideas for this target action plan are drawn from the goal-planning work of Robert S. Bailey of the Center for Creative Leadership, Greensboro, North Carolina.

DEVELOPING UNIT STRATEGIES

Having shown how emerging businesses can analyze their environments and their capabilities to develop companywide strategies and how to translate those strategies into goals for the company and its units, we turn now to developing strategies within those individual units. Think of a series of linking pins, where the goals and strategies of each unit must be consistent with the strategies of the next higher unit. Emerging companies may have three or four unit levels, and large companies may have many more, but in every case strategies at the unit level are linked both upward and downward throughout the organization. After studying this chapter, you should be able to

- understand the relationship between the goal-setting process and the development of unit strategies;
- recognize the major parts of each of the unit strategies;
- explain the importance of each part of the unit strategies;
- realize the need for consistency among the parts of the plan; and
- understand the importance of specificity in the plan.

179

Once the firm's goals have been set, unit strategies can be developed. A unit strategy is a plan of action indicating how managers within a given unit area go about achieving near-term goals. Figure 10.1 incorporates the role of unit strategies into the goal-planning model. Recall that company goals must first be prescribed for the relevant planning horizon and the near term. Then managers in each unit area can develop relevant horizon and near-term goals for their areas. With these unit-level goals firmly in mind, managers then consider unit strategies that are appropriate for each area and are consistent with both unit-level goals and overall company goals. For example, managers in the marketing department will look at the overall business goals, determine marketing's role in achieving those goals, and then set unit goals for the marketing area. They will then develop a set of marketing strategies to achieve those goals, ensuring that the marketing strategy meshes with the firm's overall strategy.

Once unit strategies are in place, managers in each area can refine their relevant goals. Each group within an area creates its particular target goals and target action plans. It should be clear that unit strategies cannot be viewed independently of, or in isolation from, goal development.

FIGURE 10.1 RELATIONSHIP BETWEEN GOALS AND STRATEGIES

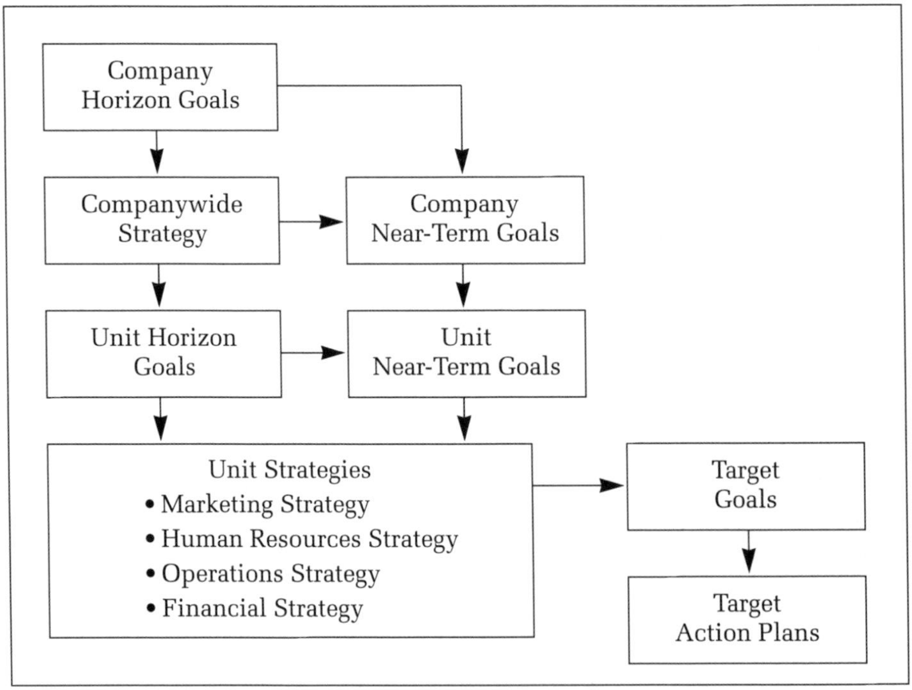

Issues that must be addressed as a prerequisite to writing the actual business plan fall into four general categories: marketing, operations, human resources, and financing. This chapter focuses on the strategic nature of the issues, and Chapter 11 discusses the actual writing of the plan.

MARKETING STRATEGY

A company's marketing strategy must be detailed enough to help the owner or manager establish, for example, how many salespersons to hire, the type and amount of advertising to use, the appropriate product mix, and pricing and selling strategies that make the most sense. The strategic plan may not answer specific questions, but it should set forth general guidelines. And it should be sufficiently detailed to easily distinguish the business from its competitors. Further, it should help employees identify and understand their relative roles in accomplishing the firm's objectives.

The Target Market Segment

Perhaps the most important marketing issue for new and emerging businesses is the determination of the market segment to be served. A significant cause of failures among emerging businesses is that they attempt to be everything to everyone. Marketing dollars are spread too thin and are therefore often wasted. If a company is trying to reach all the customers it possibly can, few will be properly served.

Defining a market segment does not mean that customers outside that segment are unwelcome. It only means they will not receive strategic attention; that is, they will not receive primary emphasis. If customers outside the defined segment purchase the firm's goods or services, that's fine. If enough customers outside the target market purchase from the company, the target market may need to be redefined. But the point is this: There will never be enough marketing dollars, so by targeting more specific segments, managers can do a better job of marketing and can serve customers better.

Consider the following example. Although many people buy waterbeds, most customers are either teenagers or adults under 30. Targeting this market limits radio advertising to rock stations and limits TV advertising to certain shows. Newspaper ads can be placed on pages most read by those who are 15 to 30 years old. Marketing dollars can also be concentrated into time/media combinations that hit the target audience most directly. Waterbed styles that are ordered most frequently by the target market are stocked and other styles special ordered, which limits inventory while still giving most of the customers immediate service.

Product Mix

The overall strategy of the company largely determines the product mix, important for all small companies but especially so for new and emerging businesses. Because these businesses are often strapped for cash, owners must decide the breadth and depth of the product line carried. Even large companies wrestle with this issue. Apple Computer, for example, announced in 1998 that it was dropping its hand-held computer; the success of the product was questionable, and the resources to support it were needed elsewhere. Smaller growth-oriented firms may need to determine if a full product line is critical to their growth and success or whether manufacturing a more narrow line will yield a higher return on investment.

Retailers may struggle with how many different brands to carry because it affects how many vendors they have to deal with, how much shelf space each product gets, and how cooperative advertising dollars are used. Product mix decisions even include such things as after-sale service, delivery policies, and store layout.

Pricing

A firm's pricing strategy is important for two reasons. The first relates to image. Part of the overall image of the firm and its product line or service comes from the price of the product or service, so obviously a relationship between price and quality exists. But the actual relationship is sometimes not as important as the perceived relationship. Most people perceive higher-priced goods to be better whether they are or not. Aspirin is a good example. FDA regulations require all aspirin to have the same active ingredients. Any brand differences are in either the coatings or the bonding agents. Yet millions, encouraged by advertising, are convinced that the national brands are worth the substantial difference in price.

In many cases, the higher-priced product *is* the better-quality product. Pennsylvania House stands out as a premier-quality brand of furniture. Cadillac, Mercedes, and Volvo carry distinctive automobile images and distinctive prices. Ben & Jerry's ice cream and Hummel figurines are other examples where price and quality are both high and well accepted.

The second reason pricing strategy is important relates to margins. One business may sell at low prices in hopes that high volume will offset low margins. Others, such as high-quality furniture stores, will depend on high margins to offset obviously lower volume. The pricing strategy depends on the elasticity of the product's demand. That is, if prices are raised by 10 percent, will total revenue increase or decrease? What will be the effect if competitors raise their prices 10 percent?

Some emerging businesses have carefully used price as a key competitive point to attract customers. Consider the case of Gateway Computers, which builds quality PCs that have become the computer of choice for many businesses and individuals. Customers order directly from Gateway, and each computer is built to the customer's specifications. Gateway delivers directly to the customer, generally within a week. By eliminating the traditional retailer, Gateway has been able to offer a well-respected machine at an attractive price.

Neither high nor low pricing is necessarily advocated, but some specific strategy should be adopted. Managers should carefully determine which type of pricing strategy works best for their firm; and sometimes a combination strategy may be used. In retail, a high-end pricing strategy may be used with most of the product line, while loss leaders are used to attract customers to the store. Manufacturing companies, such as Trek, Specialized, or Cannondale, offer some bicycle models that are high quality and high priced because they know that buyers are quality conscious and not overly concerned with price. Bikes of lower price and quality are purposely made for first-time, usually price conscious, buyers. Although the margins for lower-priced bikes may not be as high as margins for the better bikes, customers who purchase lower-priced models may later move up to the higher-priced ones.

Promotion

Promotion refers to the approaches a business takes to communicate the value of its products and services to its target market. Promotion can be done through advertising, personal selling, sales promotions, point-of-purchase displays, packaging, and even direct marketing through the Internet. The key for emerging businesses is to determine which promotional method best communicates with its target market. For example, a firm that manufactures products that are sold to other businesses will often use one-on-one personal selling and trade shows. This makes sense because building relationships and rapport are key. Once relationships are established, however, repeat orders may be done by mail or fax. Retail firms may use print, radio, or television advertising. Increasingly, firms are finding the Internet to be an excellent method for reaching customers. Virtually all publicly held companies and many emerging companies put their annual reports and product information on the Web.

Managers must determine how much money to budget for promotional activities. Despite trade-offs, the value of promotion as a marketing strategy must be clearly understood. The best products or services in the world can fail if potential customers are unaware that the business offers them. Budgets must also consider the different types of promotion available and the cost-effectiveness of each given the nature of the product and the target market.

Two caveats should be noted regarding promotional budgets. First, companies should avoid doing a little of everything; the growing business is better off concentrating its promotional efforts to reach its specific target market rather than taking a "shotgun approach" aimed at hitting every possible consumer. Second, companies should avoid placing a too-stringent financial limit on their promotional budgets. While promotion may seem to contribute little to the immediate bottom line, it is critical for the growing business.

Selling Strategy

The selling strategy a company adopts ties in closely with the image of the company because it's affected by whether a high-quality or a low-quality image is to be projected. You need only count the number of salespeople to differentiate between the self-service store and the full-service store.

Store layout is also a part of selling strategy. A store whose aisles are cluttered with merchandise that is buried or out of reach projects a different image than one with wide aisles and easily accessible merchandise.

Selling strategy depends on the target market. Sophisticated and prosperous customers may prefer personal attention when buying clothes, depend on in-home decorators when purchasing home furnishings, and want an expert to recommend art objects for their living room. Those not interested in these expensive frills may want to browse, try on clothes without being hassled by a salesclerk, or pick out their own home furnishings from the selection on the sales floor.

Selling strategy is at least as important to a manufacturing firm as it is to retail stores and is especially critical for launching a new firm. Should the manufacturer attempt to market the product directly, using a company sales force? Should manufacturer's representatives be used? Should the firm only manufacture the product, relying totally on a marketing company for distribution? Or should the owner of a manufacturing firm license the product to someone else to manufacture? Because the product can reach the final customer in a variety of ways, emerging businesses have to decide where to best allocate their resources to keep up with demand while controlling costs.

Two of the most important factors affecting selling strategy for small firms are the up-front investment and the day-to-day costs. A new firm that manufactures a single product may be forced to use a manufacturer's representative because of the high unit cost associated with an in-house sales force. The initial cost of hiring salespeople is prohibitive if a wide geographical area is being targeted. In new retail situations, day-to-day costs may be the overriding factor. Stories abound of retail stores that, in the interests of quality and personal service, staff their stores with too many clerks and find later that their wage and salary costs are excessive. Profile 10.1 is an example.

Many other short-run tactical or operational issues arise in selling, such as commissioned versus salaried salespeople, appropriate attitudes among the salesforce, and part-time versus full-time workers. All of these issues—and others as well—are part of the overall marketing strategy that owners must address in their strategic planning process.

Distribution

Distribution is of primary concern to manufacturing firms; the decision regarding distribution methods is how to get the product into the hands of the final user. In some companies, the product is sold directly from the manufacturer to the customer. Examples include large industrial equipment and the increasing use by consumer product manufacturers such as Gateway or Dell computers. In more cases, however, it

PROFILE 10.1

ANTIQUES UNLIMITED

Bill and Sandy Houlihan opened their dream business, an antiques mall called Antiques Unlimited. They sensed antiques dealers wanted a year-round showroom where they could exhibit their wares without hiring salespeople. Bill and Sandy rented space to dealers in a large building they owned and provided all salesfloor personnel, who floated from area to area monitoring and assisting customers. Bill and Sandy agreed to provide one salesclerk for every five booths or every 1,200 square feet.

Their agreement was beneficial for the dealers but a "killer" for the Houlihans. Although sometimes all salespeople were busy, far more times the only people in the mall were the clerks. There was a limit to how much dusting, arranging, and bookkeeping they could do.

Attempting to renegotiate the agreement with dealers, the Houlihans encountered resistance from the dealers of small but expensive antiques, who were concerned about shoplifting. Furniture dealers, on the other hand, were not overly concerned. The problem was partially resolved when the Houlihans agreed that the store would be fully staffed on weekends and other days or times when traffic was expected to be heavy. At other times, one clerk would have to suffice for every seven booths or 2,000 square feet. Further, they agreed to install lockable glass cases for small antiques, which allowed customers to look at their leisure without risk to the dealers of shoplifting.

makes sense to use one or more intermediaries such as wholesalers and retailers, whereby the manufacturer sells the product to a few wholesalers who, in turn, sell the product to many, many retailers. Using intermediaries on the whole is much more efficient than trying to distribute the products directly.

Service firms—plumbers, accountants, and printers, for example— also have to be concerned with distribution. Here, the issues are the number of locations, the size of the operation, and the number of staff available in each location.

OPERATIONS STRATEGY

Operations issues affect all kinds of firms; inventory, for example, is a strategic issue in both manufacturing and retail businesses as are purchasing and scheduling; and layout too is a concern for both retail stores and manufacturing firms. Operations strategy covers decisions related to the manufacture of goods or provision of services and to the facilities issues associated with them.

Facilities

Strategic decisions about facilities are necessarily integrated with marketing and financial strategies. Major investments in facilities, for example, may be required to meet increasing demand, but investing thousands of dollars in plant and equipment may take resources away from marketing that will be needed to sell the very products produced in the expanded facilities. Or consider this. Managers of a growing firm find they have an insufficient number of trainers to instruct dealers how to best sell and service their product, so they decide to hire two more trainers and add $20,000 of audiovisual equipment for training. However, if they spend the $20,000 to buy the equipment, they won't have enough funds left to hire both of the new trainers. They can have either the new equipment, or they can have two new trainers, but they can't have both. This dilemma is known as opportunity cost—committing to one action precludes committing to another. It's a problem that affects many resource-driven strategic decisions, but it is also often prevalent in issues related to facilities and operations.

Because facilities use extraordinary amounts of capital, the growth-oriented business owner must carefully project how large the firm's operations are expected to be or are expected to grow in the foreseeable future. One of the most important decisions to be made is the acquisition of the appropriate amount and type of space for the firm's operations. Thus, forecasting sales is critical to facilities decisions.

Two strategic errors are common in decisions about space, either of which can adversely impact an emerging firm's ability to compete in the long run. The first is overcapacity. The owner assumes the firm will grow quickly and leases or buys more capacity than the firm can use or afford. Later, the firm is in trouble because of the financial drain caused by the overcapacity. The second error is acquiring insufficient space, which leads to undercapacity. Operations quickly become so cramped that they are severely inefficient; with no room for expansion, the firm must relocate. Retail stores often lose customers when they relocate, and for manufacturers the expense of relocating equipment and retrofitting a new facility may create financial difficulties.

Another space-related issue is the type of space needed. Unfortunately, in many cases the small business starts out by using the most easily available space rather than the most appropriate space. An entrepreneur starts a home-based business and stays there even though better space is sorely needed; a budding retailer decides to open a shop near her home when space is available across town in a well-traveled shopping center; a manufacturer accepts space in an old warehouse and then finds that the costs of remodeling and rewiring are excessive.

The key to space acquisition is finding a location that has enough space yet not too much. There are no hard-and-fast rules. A rough guide for slower-growing firms is to acquire space that is 15 to 20 percent too large or that may be fully utilized within a year to 18 months. Emerging or fast-growing firms should assume that growth will continue into the near future and acquire space that is considerably larger than currently needed, thus ensuring available space and offsetting the near-term undercapacity problem. Although this strategy does present an immediate overcapacity problem, it is not as serious a problem as being under capacity a short while after moving into the facility. The extra space is a necessary hedge at a relatively small cost.

Make-or-Buy Decisions

The make-or-buy decision is another important strategic operations decision. It involves a great deal of money and is irreversible—at least in the short run. For a manufacturing firm, the choices are to

- manufacture all products in-house;
- manufacture one or more prime products in-house and purchase other products finished, perhaps in packaging bearing the company name;

- assemble some or all products from finished components and package them; or
- produce nothing, contract all production, do only packaging or perhaps not even that, and be responsible only for marketing the finished product.

Several factors influence the decision, and the firm's financial condition is certainly one. A business that is not able to invest large sums of money in manufacturing facilities may be forced to contract most of its production. Insufficient space may also force a firm to contract some of its production. On the other hand, a desire for quality may lead a firm to keep all of its production in-house. Lower production costs may also be a reason to produce components in-house if the firm can make them for less than they could be purchased outside. In some cases, higher quality or lower costs may not be as important as the availability of goods. If components must be purchased from suppliers that are unreliable in meeting delivery dates, the company may be forced into producing its own components.

Some firms are taking the make-or-buy decision to new levels. They are creating what are called virtual organizations, in which the firm either makes nothing or only a core set of products or engages in only certain processes with all the rest outsourced. Outsourcing minimizes the investment the firm makes and limits its activities to only those things it does best. The virtual organization is very small—only a skeleton of what most companies are. The outsourcing allows it to appear to produce without the high fixed cost of plant and equipment.

Vendor Selection

An issue being increasingly considered by both large and emerging small businesses is vendor selection. Many large companies have switched from using several vendors who each provide perhaps 20 percent of the firm's component needs to using a single vendor who satisfies the firm's entire demand for the product. In the former system, the firm uses multiple vendors as a hedge against one or more of them becoming unreliable. In the latter case, usually used in conjunction with a just-in-time inventory system, the firm contracts with a single vendor who agrees to provide the inventory precisely when needed and at a competitive price. The contracting firm works hand-in-hand with the vendor to ensure that problems don't arise. Smaller companies can't use just-in-time inventory to the same extent as large firms because they don't have the clout to ensure that a supplier meets all their demands. However, the basic concepts of this method are still viable. Reducing the number of suppliers makes the business more vulnerable to the remaining supplier, but it can also result in increased quality if only the best supplier is used and can sometimes also result in price breaks. In addition, the ease of working with a single supplier may offset other risks.

Finished Inventory Strategy

As well as dealing with strategies covering suppliers and raw materials, owners must also adopt a strategy for inventorying finished goods. The cost of maintaining substantial inventory must be weighed against two other factors, the first being the problem of stockouts. If the amount of inventory is kept too close to demand, any sudden changes can result in stockouts that cause a company to lose both sales and customer goodwill. In addition, maintaining minimal inventory causes both production runs and personnel needs to fluctuate, particularly true for manufacturers who produce seasonal goods. Producing inventory in the off-season allows the owner to have a more level production schedule and to avoid adding and laying off workers.

Complicating finished goods inventory even more is the cost of the inventory and its storage and the effect of that cost on the company's financial condition. Thus, managers of emerging companies must consider the trade-offs between having an inventory strategy that causes too much inventory to be held versus one that causes too little to be kept. Either error can be serious. Emerging firms, however, must carefully guard against running out of inventory because they are in a growth cycle, a situation in which stockouts can be disastrous—competitors can move in quickly and capture market share.

HUMAN RESOURCES STRATEGY

Many human resources–related issues fall more within operational policies than within the larger strategic plan. However, our focus is on major organizational issues that affect the overall business and its owners.

Employee Selection

Perhaps no strategic issue is more important for emerging businesses than the selection of competent managers and employees. Managers are responsible for both the strategic direction of the firm and its day-to-day operations, and they are critical in facilitating the company's growth. Thus, extreme care must be taken when hiring additional managers. Competent employees are the foundation for the business's growth; and even if there are no-hard-and-fast rules for choosing employees, some suggestions may help:

- Hire on the basis of ability, not friendship. Most people like to work with others when the relationship is comfortable and friendly, but skills and talent are far more important. It may be fun to work with friends, but they may not have the background and ability to contribute what's needed. In addition, it's very difficult to fire friends if they don't perform adequately. This is a significant problem in family businesses as family members may expect to be hired and promoted regardless of their contribution to the business.
- Hire to offset existing weaknesses. Frequently, the tendency is for company managers to hire those who think like them. The greater need, however, may be to hire those whose strengths offset current managerial weaknesses.
- Develop the position and then fit a person to it. Don't hire a person and then find a job to match the individual.
- Think strategy! Many people can handle day-to-day administrative duties, but finding someone with entrepreneurial capabilities who can think toward the future is considerably more difficult.
- Once an employee is chosen, the key words are train and delegate. Give the new person sufficient guidance to develop important skills and understanding of the business, and then delegate authority and responsibility. This allows the manager of the emerging business to concentrate on the overall business growth strategy rather than spending too much time with routine decision making and provides all employees with a feeling of competence and importance.

Wage and Salary Strategies

Wage and salary strategies are different from wage and salary policies. Policies deal with the technical aspects of implementing wage and salary strategies. The strategic emphasis of wage and salary issues is on items that significantly affect the overall operation of the business. One important strategic issue is whether the firm will have a high-salary or a low-salary strategy coupled with benefit packages. These are strategic issues because they can affect the firm's ability to attract and retain key qualified workers. Managers of emerging firms, struggling to save scarce cash, may decide to use a low-salary approach or even consider deferred pay. Such strategies may not be successful, especially in periods of low unemployment and high industry growth, because competitors may hire the best managers, leaving the company with only the less qualified ones, who were not selected by higher-paying competitors. On the other hand, of course, a company that uses the high-salary strategy may attract good workers but be unable to pay them while keeping prices competitive.

Similar strategic decisions must be made with lower-level employees. Hiring already-trained employees may require paying them more; it may be more costly, but the new workers can quickly become productive. Hiring untrained but lower-paid employees may save on the human resource budget but increase costs in the training budget.

The benefits issue is particularly important from a strategic standpoint as benefits don't add directly to the firm's productivity. The basic value the business gains from providing additional employee benefits may come from having a more dedicated, more loyal workforce, as demonstrated perhaps by an employee stock option plan, whereby the owner is willing to share increasing amounts of ownership in exchange for presumed increases in employee commitment and dedication to the business.

Even fast-paced, technology-oriented businesses recognize that continued success only occurs when the right people are in place. Organic Online, for example, highlighted in Profile 10.2, realizes that having talented people and treating them right is key to its development as an emerging business. As CEO Jon Nelson suggests, the need for delegating and empowering is necessary to meet the growing work demands that an emerging business faces.

FINANCIAL STRATEGY

Most analysts of business failures suggest they occur for two main reasons. One is a general lack of managerial planning. The second is the

PROFILE 10.2

Organic Online: The Company Is the People

Organic Online is a hot Internet business that creates leading-edge Web sites for big companies like McDonald's, Harley-Davidson, and Nike. Organic's success has been phenomenal: Started out of Nelson's home in 1993, the company now has 125 employees. Having developed creative Web sites for over 50 companies, Organic has prospered in the turbulent and competitive field of Internet business.

As the company grew, CEO Jon Nelson realized he couldn't do everything on his own. He had to delegate, and that meant having good people. "It's all about finding great managers and staff. I guess I'm a big wheel here, but Organic Online is not the Jon Nelson show. The company is the people. At the end of the day, we're a people company," notes Nelson. Nelson observed that in the early days of the business it was hard "delegating, empowering, and trusting. But I now know that I can't do it all. I don't even try. I just say to people, 'You be responsible.'"

Nelson works hard to build pride and motivation in his people. He offers an attractive health benefits package with coverage for employees and domestic partners. He makes personal computers available to his employees and even has bagels for them in the morning. Nelson admits that delegating is not easy for the top person of an emerging business. Yet he understands its importance. "[Delegating is] probably the biggest thing," he observes.

Source: James Kim, "Xers Mark the Spot for Success," *USA Today,* November 11, 1996, p. 3B; and www.organic.com/overview/brief/, accessed May 30, 1998.

failure to finance the business adequately. Of course, inadequate financing may be a result of poor planning! Many small businesses—and a number of emerging businesses—are undercapitalized. Often, they don't have adequate resources to weather economic downturns, and many can't take advantage of growth opportunities. Managers of emerging businesses must regularly monitor their financial position and their financial strategies.

Financial strategies used by new and emerging businesses fall into two general categories: equity strategies and debt strategies. Most businesses will use a combination of financial sources as their overall financial strategy. In many cases new businesses and often emerging businesses will rely heavily on the personal funds of the business's owners. Other combinations may include finding individual investors, venture capital, partnerships, and a variety of debt.

The amount and source of funding is an integral part of the firm's strategy because it will affect the growth potential and control of the business. For example, an owner who uses a high-debt strategy will maintain full control of the operation but will have a high debt-service expense. The high level of debt may make the company vulnerable, especially when the economy moves into a recession or the industry falls on hard times. Conversely, a company that has a high-equity strategy will have relatively less debt to service but must share some amount of profit and control with investors. Moreover, companies whose managers are very conservative may use too little of either debt or equity and thereby limit growth.

Debt Strategies

Small start-up businesses may have relatively few alternatives to a debt strategy, especially true if the start-up is a retail or service business. The options may be personal loans by the owner, loans from friends or relatives, or loans from a commercial bank. In the latter case, a percentage of equity capital is a prerequisite. For example, a firm needing $50,000 may be able to get only $35,000 from a bank; the remaining $15,000 will have to be owner's equity. Banks tend to be wary of small start-ups because so many fail. Related to bank financing is the Small Business Administration's (SBA) guaranteed loan program, under which a bank agrees to the financing but the SBA guarantees 80 percent of the loan amount for loans of $100,000 or less and guarantees 75 percent for all other loans.[1] Thus, a bank is risking only 25 to 30 percent of its funds, even though it's loaning the entire amount. This encourages a bank to work with small businesses to which they might not otherwise offer a straight commercial loan. Of course, the SBA guarantee does not in any way remove the burden of repayment from the business or its owners.

Emerging companies have a somewhat easier time tapping into debt money than start-up companies because they are already established and in a growth mode. Lenders may be willing to loan them money because they realize that emerging companies need the money to underwrite rapid growth, and lenders feel their money is safe as the industry is growing. There is a downside for emerging companies, however: Growth quickly outstrips available debt capital. Even though banks may be willing to loan emerging companies part of what they need, banks may be unwilling to loan the entire amount needed.

Equity Strategies

A variety of financing strategies fall within the area of equity financing. As before, the type of strategy chosen may be a function of what is available, although it may also be a function of the owner's overall strategic plan.

Partnerships are an obvious source of equity funding, but partnering is a strategy that the primary owner must consider carefully. This method of financing has merit in that a working partner not only provides capital but also provides additional management skills. On the other hand, taking in a partner changes the nature of the business. The primary owner is no longer the sole decision maker. Further, taking in a partner requires that the profits or losses also be shared. In some cases, a limited partner or silent partner can be found. Then decision making normally rests with the primary partner, although profits or losses must still be split with the other partners. Managers of emerging businesses must consider whether a partner will help the company grow. If there are doubts about the role a partner might play as the company continues to grow, then careful thought should precede a decision to add a partner.

A second strategy for raising equity capital is to sell stock either to individuals or to the general public through an initial public offering, or IPO. Emerging companies often sell stock to wealthy acquaintances or to individual investors, often referred to as angels, who invest in a number of high-potential businesses. Business angels can sometimes be found through a venture-funding database run by some universities or through contacts with attorneys, accountants, and stock brokers, who may be aware of individuals looking for investments. Selling stock in this manner will normally require that a business plan be prepared for investors.

Much of that information, however, can be taken from the written strategic plan. Emerging businesses that have already had some success may consider going public through an IPO, as is the case with Wilderness Sports, highlighted in Profile 10.3. An IPO is a complex process requiring assistance from investment bankers and underwriters and sometimes taking a year or more to accomplish. However, if it is successful, the IPO can bring in a substantial amount of funds.

Venture capitalists are an attractive avenue of financing for some emerging businesses. There are many varieties, each with its own preferred investments; some, for example, invest only in high-tech compa-

---

PROFILE 10.3

Wilderness Sports: Growing through an IPO

Wildnerness Sports was started in June 1992. Its retail store, in the Sacramento Sports Center, is located between Lake Tahoe and the San Francisco Bay area. Wilderness offers upper-end clothing and equipment for outdoor recreational activities; it sells and rents outdoor recreational equipment for activities ranging from backpacking and backcountry skiing to canoeing and kayaking.

The company is now online and hopes to be fully interactive soon. With the business growing and customer interest in outdoor adventures flourishing, Wildnerness has big plans for future growth. Of course, growth and big plans take money, so Wildnerness has decided to go public and offer stock for sale to the public. It is among the growing number of emerging businesses delving into an initial public offering, or IPO. Wildnerness is offering 200,000 shares of common stock for sale at $5 per share for an aggregate offering of $1 million. If successful, the cash infusion will help Wildnerness tap its special niche in the recreational market.

Source: www.wildnernesssports.com.background.html, accessed May 30, 1998; and www.ipo.com/wildnerness.asp, accessed May 30, 1998.

nies. Some venture capital firms are associated with industrial firms and only invest in companies that complement the parent firm's operations; and some venture capital firms insist on majority ownership, although most take a minority, but significant, ownership position. All venture capitalists require an extensive business plan, and they typically underwrite only about 1 percent of the companies whose plans they review.

Other Funding Strategies

Some funding sources don't fall neatly into either the debt or equity category, but they must still be considered part of financial strategy. Leasing equipment rather than purchasing it is attractive in some cases, especially when equipment has a relatively short life or may become obsolete within a few years. Although leasing may ultimately be more expensive than owning, it doesn't tie up corporate funds and eliminates the need to incur debt.

Suppliers often provide short-term inventory financing, which technically is debt financing as there is an obligation to pay. However, the payment may be made a few weeks later or, more rarely, at the end of the season.

Customers can also be a source of financing, often involving complex equipment that is specially ordered. The manufacturer requires partial payment on order, with the remainder due on delivery. The manufacturer has thereby shifted part of the financial burden away from the firm to the customer, thus reducing debt.

The Need for a Plan

Although there are several sources and possible strategies for financing, remember the underlying importance of developing a financial strategy, in part for building a business plan that can be taken to lenders or equity sources. Financing should never be done ad hoc; owners should always be aware of the various sources and uses of funds. The overall strategic plan must include financial strategy to allow the effective merging of financial strategy, marketing strategy, human resources strategy, and operations strategy.

THE CONSULTANT'S VIEWPOINT

Consultants are seldom called in to assess all functional or unit strategies. It is more likely, for example, that they will be asked to examine the marketing strategy and make recommendations. Or perhaps they will be called in to help design a financial strategy. They may be asked to study inventory strategies with the goal of making the company more efficient.

In working with unit strategies, consultants must keep the big picture in mind. Even if the assignment is marketing related, the marketing strategy must mesh with the overall strategy of the firm and with the other unit strategies. Indeed, this is why many senior project consulting teams are structured with team members from a variety of different business majors such as finance, accounting, marketing, and management. Individual professional consultants working with a company must be careful not to let tunnel vision in a specific discipline cloud the big picture for the firm.

Unit strategies must be written down no matter how tempting to simply discuss the strategies and be done with it. It is far better that each unit manager is forced to write the strategy in some detail to reduce the chances that key aspects of the plan will be missed. It also affords the opportunity for the written document to be shared with others in the organization that will be affected by it.

A final point is to again note the difference between a unit strategy and a policy. A consultant may, indeed, be called in to assess a policy but may find that it is the unit strategy rather than a policy that is incorrect. For example, suppose a company is having difficulty with credit collections. The business owner may ask a consultant to analyze the company's collection policies. The consultant may find that the collection policy—how the company goes about collecting debts—is OK. What's wrong is the credit strategy, including deciding whether credit should be offered. Perhaps the company sells a product for which it really makes sense for customers to pay in cash. If so, it shouldn't have a collection policy at all because it shouldn't have any credit sales. Perhaps replacing in-house credit with bank credit cards makes more sense; the fees charged by credit card companies may be more than offset by the bad debts on in-house accounts.

DISCUSSION QUESTIONS

1. How will the marketing strategy of a discount firm differ from that of a top-of-the-line firm?
2. How does a firm's pricing strategy relate to its image?
3. Is it possible to have a manufacturing strategy that is relatively independent of the other parts of a firm's strategy?
4. How does human resources strategy relate to marketing strategy? To financial strategy?
5. Determine the overall strategy of a small manufacturing firm in your area. Then look at each unit strategy. Do they match?

NOTES

1. SBA terms, www.firstsecuritybank.com/sbaterms.htm, accessed, August 14, 1998.

Writing the Plan

By this time, you should have a good feel for what goes into a strategic plan. You realize the need for both an external analysis of the firm's environment and an objective analysis of the firm's strengths and weaknesses. You understand the nature of distinctive competencies, growth strategy, goals, and unit strategies. But one more task remains: to put the analysis into a written document that can be read by the people with a vested interest in how the firm competes. With this in mind, when you finish this chapter, you should

- have a good understanding of what an actual strategic plan looks like and
- be able to write a plan that fulfills the purposes discussed throughout the book.

This chapter reviews the items to be included in the strategic plan and discusses the actual format and writing. The strategic planning model was divided into three phases: phase 1, providing the vision and mission of the business; phase 2, the analysis; and phase 3, the actions necessary to develop the strategy. The final step of the action phase is the actual writing of the plan.

WHY WRITE THE PLAN?

Small business owners frequently make the dangerous assumption that a plan can be stored in their mind and still give them needed direction and guidance. Although the strategic plan is primarily an instrument for guiding the owner, others also read it; employees, for example, can benefit from an awareness of where the business is headed. For emerging businesses and even some new ventures, investors too are keenly interested in reading the plan; and at times, suppliers or even potential customers may want to read it. Even though some items in the written plan may seem trite or self-evident to the owner, they may be necessary for others. New and emerging businesses may need to share their plan or portions of their plan with investors, lenders, key suppliers, or perhaps even other businesses that might be partners in a strategic alliance.

Reasonably specific detail should be included—as much detail as confidentiality allows. Although details may seem unnecessary, remember that a second key use of the plan is to review progress. The more specific the plan, the better progress can be evaluated. Less obvious is the motivational effect of putting the plan on paper. The owner and employees are likely to be more committed to a plan if that plan has been put on paper and shared with others. Consider Reder Electronics in Profile 11.1.

THE STRATEGIC PLAN FORMAT

Figure 11.1 shows the format for a strategic plan. This is followed by a detailed discussion of the format.

PROFILE 11.1

Reder Electronics

Reder Electronics sets forth a strategic plan at the beginning of each fiscal year that specifies relevant aspects of its environment, presents an assessment of its internal strengths and weaknesses, and lays out the firm's goals clearly. A strategy for the year is then presented that will be used to achieve the goals. The plan is not filed away, never to be seen again; rather, it is a working document, referenced and reexamined regularly. Scott Reder feels that such checks are critical and encourages quarterly reviews.

During these progress checks, Reder compares both the internal analysis and the external assessment in the plan to the current situation. If necessary, a plan may be changed. Remember, a plan is not etched in stone. The important thing, according to Reder, is that the process he follows allows the business to "note where we have been and how far we have to go to attain either the goals we set for ourselves or the new goals that have developed since that writing."

Sometimes the quarterly analysis is favorable and encouraging. Sometimes it isn't. But the reexamination procedure allows Reder to know where the company is compared with where he wants it to be and then allows him to focus on corrective action.

The Vision and Mission Statements

The written vision and mission statements (see Chapter 3) need be no more than one or two paragraphs, although some may be a bit longer. The vision statement should include what the owner wants the company to be at some time in the future. The mission statement must lay out the general direction of the company and describe the firm's product line or groups of

FIGURE 11.1   STRATEGIC PLAN FORMAT

I. Vision statement

II. Mission statement
   A. Product line or services provided
   B. Philosophy of the business

III. The business and its environment
   A. General environment characteristics
   B. Industry environment and competition
   C. Location description

IV. Distinctive competencies

V. Growth strategies and goals
   A. Company-level strategies
   B. Company goals
      1. Horizon goals
      2. Near-term goals

VI. Unit-level goals and strategies
   A. Marketing
      1. Target market
      2. Product mix strategy
      3. Pricing strategy
      4. Promotion and selling strategy
      5. Distribution strategy
   B. Operations
      1. Facilities
      2. Make-or-buy decisions
      3. Lease/purchase of equipment
      4. Vendor selection
   C. Human resources
      1. Employment strategy
      2. Promote from within versus hiring outside managers
      3. Wage/salary/benefits strategy
   D. Financing
      1. Debt/equity strategy
      2. Capital sourcing strategy
      3. Growth/stability strategy
      4. Financial projections

VII. Target goals and target action plan

product lines. It should also briefly discuss the owner's business philosophy. And it should be specific enough to let the reader assess how the business operates and how its culture, tone, or climate appears to the public.

The Business and Its Environment

This section of the plan is a broad overview of the business designed to give potential readers a feel for the business and its operating environment. It need not be excessively detailed but should provide the reader with a solid understanding of the firm and the key dynamics affecting its operation.

Initially, characteristics of the general environment should be discussed because general environmental factors affect all businesses. Even so, note whether the company is a wholesale, manufacturing, retail, or service business.

Next, provide a fairly detailed discussion of the industry in which the firm competes. It should include the industry's sensitivity to the economy, the intensity of competition, the nature of competition (price versus quality versus product differentiation), and the size of the total market. Specific information on competitors should follow. Estimate each competitor's market share and other significant competitive factors. Include any additional relevant information about key competitors. Taken together, the industry and competitors' data should provide a reasonably clear idea of the size of the market and the degree of turbulence to expect in the industry that should give the reader an idea of where the business fits within the industry.

Discuss the general location of the business, which may include overall community characteristics as well as comments on the business's specific location. The key here is to include information that will be valuable for comparison later. Include such items as the unemployment rate in the local community, the general outlook for the community, the relative location of competitors, and the strengths and weaknesses of the company's location within the community.

Distinctive Competencies

Explain the company's distinctive competencies, with the degree of detail dependent on the intended audience. If the primary readers are inside the organization, a fairly specific rendering of distinctive competencies should be included to give employees management's perception of the firm's key strengths, which may also be useful if lenders or other investors will be reading the plan. On the other hand, if suppliers, customers, or others outside the firm have access to the plan, then a more conservative, less detailed presentation of the distinctive competencies should be given so as not to tip off competitors about proprietary information.

Growth Strategies and Goals

This section lays out in more detail the direction in which the firm is headed. It also focuses on more specific goals, both for the business as a whole and for the units within the business.

Growth strategies.   The strategies that the business will pursue in order to grow should be explained well, including their justification. Remember that a growth strategy is an overall, general plan or approach for running the firm in response to its external and internal conditions (refer to Chapter 8). The description of the individual strategies in the plan must be detailed enough to make their precise nature clear.

Company goals.   While the mission and vision statements let readers know where the business is headed and growth strategies prescribe a general business approach for getting there, company goals enable the reader to see the specific achievements or results the owner expects the business to reach. Company goals covering both the horizon and near term should be included. The two time frames should be presented so that readers can clearly see the relationship between the near-term goals and the broader horizon goals.

As noted in Chapter 9, horizon goals are oriented toward the overall planning horizon, so these goals are stated in broad terms. Near-term goals concentrate on the next business operating period and require greater precision, detail, and specificity. Horizon and near-term goals are fundamental, critical elements in the written plan. Goal statements are one of the primary factors that outside readers focus on in assessing the business, its scope of activities, and the plausibility of its intended direction. In addition, near-term goals become the key benchmarks for monitoring and evaluating business operations. Their effects on internal direction and control, as well as on external perceptions of the business, are quite significant.

Unit Goals and Strategies

Once company goals have been written into the plan, enumerate the unit-level goals and strategies for both horizon and near-term time frames. Unit goals are written in the same manner as company goals except that they focus on issues relevant to a functional area. Of course, unit goals must mesh with and complement each other and relate and support the fulfillment of broader company goals.

Once unit-level goals are written, add statements of unit strategies relevant to the achievement of these goals. Four areas of unit strategies have been stressed: marketing, operations, human resources, and finance. Although these are not necessarily an all-inclusive list of concerns, they do represent the key unit areas for most emerging businesses.

Marketing.   At least five items should be identified as part of marketing strategy. Address each separately in order to have a clear understanding of the firm's total marketing strategy. In general, these strategy decisions will be led, or primarily determined by, the unit goals.

The target market should specifically identify the primary customers of the business. Note the demographic makeup of the target market, including age ranges, socioeconomic status, customer location if relevant, and any other distinguishing characteristics (refer to Chapter 4). It may be helpful to include target market A and target market B, where the A group includes those in the primary target market and the B group includes those in an important but secondary category.

The product mix strategy consists of a description of the general products carried by the firm, including whether the products are considered top of the line, moderately priced, or economy priced. It should indicate the breadth and depth of the product line and if special orders are accepted or encouraged. It should also indicate whether the firm intends to increase its product mix over time, maintain the mix, or phase out portions of the product line.

The pricing strategy should follow the product strategy. Very simply, it should state whether the pricing strategy is to price higher than, competitive with, or lower than competitors. It may include more specific information, such as "Our pricing strategy is to consistently price 15 percent below the competition and to honor competitors' prices in those cases in which their prices are lower than ours."

The promotion strategy is certainly one of the key aspects of the overall marketing strategy. Chapter 10 suggests the importance of determining an overall promotion strategy, budgeting for it correctly, and staying with that strategy. It is very important that the selected strategy be defined as specifically as possible in order to serve as a control later on. Write down the promotional strategy, because writing encourages consistency.

The promotional plan includes the total budgeted amount to be spent on advertising and other promotional activities; a month-by-month breakdown of the annual promotional budget; a description of the media to be used; the frequency of advertising; whether (and which) advertising agencies will be used; the nature of the advertising; and the image to be conveyed. Each of these items should be laid out in as much detail as possible and then regularly reviewed. A haphazard promotion strategy can confuse customers and allow promotion resources to be used inefficiently. At the very least, the written strategy should eliminate spur-of-the-moment acquiescence to some aggressive ad salesperson who walks in the door.

The distribution strategy should have been determined as a result of earlier analysis. Write it down clearly so that readers inside and outside the business can understand and evaluate it easily. Include the types of distribution channels used, the method of accessing those channels, the reasons those particular channels are used, and the impact the distribution system should have on sales. Again, the reason for writing this on paper is not only to have it available for others to see but also for the business owner to be able to review it at a later date. As a business grows, the most effective and efficient method of distribution may change. At one stage in a manufacturing business, for example, a manufacturer's representative may be the most efficient method of distribution. But as the business grows, an in-house salesperson plus an on-the-road commissioned sales force may be more effective and more efficient. In some situations, the opposite case can be made: The company sales force introduces the product, and a manufacturer's representative takes over once the product becomes established and well known in the industry.

Operations.   Strategies relating to operations tend to be more stable than those relating to marketing because they often deal with fixed assets rather than annual expenses. Far more analysis is involved in determining an initial operations strategy, and equal care must be taken when changing it. Typical of these decisions is the strategy covering facilities.

Operations strategies are much less frequently changed than are some of the others, but it's still wise to write them down on paper for employees and other key people to read. Also, operations strategies serve as the basis for developing cohesive policies to guide day-to-day actions within the core part of the business.

For product-related firms, make-or-buy decisions are key parts of operations strategies and should be clearly delineated in the strategic planning document. Included here are statements declaring whether the firm, for example, plans to be a full manufacturer, an assembler, a distributor, or some combination of the above. These decisions will typically also answer the make-or-buy questions, but more specifications should be included if the firm makes part of its components and purchases the rest outside. In the Joy's Toys Company example in Profile 11.2, the overall

---

PROFILE 11.2

Joy's Toys Company

Operations Strategy

Joy's Toys Company's production strategy is to do all assembly work on its stuffed animals and produce the clothes for all the models. Parts for the animals will be purchased from reputable suppliers only, thereby reducing the need for 100 percent inspection of purchased materials. Cloth for the skin will be purchased ready to cut. Stuffing will be purchased in the largest quantities that inventory space will allow to take advantage of volume discounts. Hard pieces (eyes, noses, and buttons) will be standardized as much as possible throughout all models to reduce both ordering and inventory costs.

Attempts will be made to retain workers as long as possible to reduce assembly defects. Cutting machines are scheduled to be replaced on a rotating basis beginning the last quarter of this year, with one machine replaced each of the next six quarters.

If market research indicates that sales of the newest models will continue to expand, new facilities for storage of finished inventory will be necessary by 2001. Therefore, preliminary plans for the building should be developed by the end of the second quarter of 2000.

Cost reductions will be necessary throughout the next several quarters, especially on the older models. Discussions will be held with marketing personnel on how to encourage distributors to submit larger orders so as to increase the size of production runs.

operations strategy combines some longer-range strategies with some shorter-term ones. This is perfectly acceptable because the overall strategy should be reviewed at least semiannually anyway. The strategy statement serves as a later check against whether the marketing department did in fact cooperate successfully, whether the market research did in fact show increased sales projections, and whether the building plan was in fact completed.

Make-or-buy decisions should be included in the overall operations strategy. Joy's Toys consciously decided to purchase most material from reputable suppliers rather than manufacture the cloth, eyes, buttons, and the like. This doesn't mean the company should proceed in this manner forever. In later strategy reviews, a decision might be made to manufacture the eyes and buttons in-house, which would be a significant change in strategy, however, and a decision that would be made only after careful study.

Leasing rather than purchasing equipment is a decision in which individuals both inside and outside the business may have an interest. Those inside the business may be interested because of the ramifications of the decision on service, equipment replacement schedules, warranties, and so on. Those outside the business may be interested because of the financial ramifications. Investors and lenders may want to know the impact of leasing on the cash flow of the company as well as on the balance sheet and income statements. In other words, purchasing equipment outright may require significant debt, but the equipment appears as an asset on the balance sheet. If the equipment is leased, the initial expenditure and debt are not as significant, but lease payments become a substantial expense.

Vendor strategies should be included too. The primary issue is whether to have a single source or multiple sources for particular supplies. Having a single source suggests larger quantities, thereby opening up the possibility of quantity discounts. On the other hand, having multiple sources is a lower-risk strategy, assuming all suppliers can meet quality standards.

Human resources. Many policies fall within the human resource function—testing, interviewing, evaluation, and termination. Some human resources strategies, however, must be considered and included in the written strategic plan.

First is employment strategy. Of particular importance are sources of managers and line workers and the method of hiring them. For example, it may be part of the strategy to hire only college graduates from accredited business schools. Some large firms hire liberal arts graduates, whom they then train in-house. Other firms hire only experienced workers, thus alleviating the need for all but orientation training once workers are hired.

The second aspect of human resources strategy is promotion. This may appear to be more of a policy than a strategy, but it fits the definition of strategy because it can determine the future effectiveness of the company's people. The plan should indicate whether the firm typically promotes from within or hires managers from outside. A case can be made either way, but the strategy should be communicated to interested people, including employees.

A third strategy issue to be delineated is compensation, which, of course, must be kept relatively broad to avoid internal problems. But such items as a bonus plan, insurance benefits, company cars, and stock options should be included. If the company has a history of paying higher-than-competitive wages, this should be noted and periodically reviewed. Any other items in the wage and salary area that might make the company more attractive than its competitors should also be included.

Financing.   Much of the financial strategy is more detailed in a business plan used for getting financing than it is in the strategic plan. However, it is important to include major factors of the financial strategy in the strategic plan both as a guide for future direction and as a control.

A major portion of financial strategy deals with debt versus equity. In new businesses, a default strategy may be followed—whatever strategy is successful will be used. The most successful strategy may be the only strategy available.

An emerging business typically has more options. Some owners prefer to rely totally on internally generated funds, taking on little or no additional equity or debt financing. This may limit growth, of course, but it's a viable strategy. Others may rely primarily on debt financing, and still others on additional equity financing or on a combination of debt and equity financing. As we have said many times, the concern is not what is included in the strategy but that the strategy be presented in written form to allow reading and review.

Capital sources to be tapped should be listed as these will change over time. Numerous sources are available, including banks, venture capitalists, state and federal loan programs, and suppliers. If the firm is to use a combination of these sources, a rough estimation of the relative proportion of each should be stated.

An additional item that should be included in discussing sources of capital is the rate of growth the emerging firm wants to achieve. Will the firm use all available sources of financing to the maximum in order to achieve the highest possible growth, or will growth be a function of the amount of financing that can be obtained with minimum risk? The growth question must be answered early on in the strategic planning process because it affects nearly all other areas of the business. Growth preferences are also covered in the vision section and in the company strategy sections.

Financial projections are one of the most important parts of the strategic plan and the most important part of an investment-oriented business plan. Lenders or venture capitalists want to see monthly or quarterly projections of income statements for one or two years along with quarterly or annual projections for up to five years. In emerging businesses, a cash flow projection is perhaps even more important than the income statement projection simply because the manager of an emerging business is often strapped for cash and constantly needs to be aware of relative cash inflows and outflows. It is not uncommon for a small business to be in serious trouble, even though it is making a profit, because the outflows of cash necessarily precede the inflows. This is especially true if the business deals in credit or does work for federal, state, or local government, which is often slow in paying for goods or services. Similarly, the balance sheet should be completed for the year-end of each of the next several years (refer to Chapter 6 for a review of various financial statements).

Target Goals and Target Action Plans

Although it is important to write down target goals and target action plans, they are so specific that they are typically presented in a separate document. Readers outside the company will find the detail of these areas unnecessary for their purposes. For the owner and employees, however, they offer daily guidance. (Details about target goals and target action plans are presented in Chapter 9.) Remember that because target goals and action plans are short run, they need to be flexible and adaptable.

SHARING THE PLAN

Once the task of writing the strategic plan is complete, what should managers do with it? Of course, it must be communicated to key people in the firm (although many of them were no doubt involved in developing the plan). Debate arises over how widely to distribute the plan. Some argue that sharing the plan provides employees with a keener sense of where the business is headed and thereby improves their dedication and motivation. The same logic could apply to key suppliers or those with whom the business is building strategic links or alliances. If the workforce is small and viewed as stable and loyal, it's a good idea to share at least part of the plan if not all of it with everyone. Similarly, if alliances are strong and enduring, sharing the plan or key portions of it makes sense.

The other side of the debate deals with the real need for security and the protection of sensitive information. For example, there is some risk that an employee may take the information from the plan and either join a competitor or start a competing business. By the same token, other businesses may use information from the plan to their competitive advantage. In these cases, excerpts from the plan may be the preferred route. Employees, for example, could be given the goal section of the plan, and more sensitive items shared only with top management. The complete plan or portions of it may need to be shown to investors, suppliers, or key customers, but it's a good idea not to show sensitive information to outside groups unless it's specifically required.

THE CONSULTANT'S VIEWPOINT

As consultants work with managers of emerging businesses, they should encourage managers to differentiate between a business plan used when financing is needed and the strategic plan that is used to guide the company's performance. The strategic plan has a different flavor or tone than does the business plan, which is written in an upbeat, optimistic style. The purpose of the business plan is to generate interest in providing capital to the firm. The strategic plan, on the other hand, is written objectively and is for the benefit of people inside the firm; it shouldn't be glossy or unduly optimistic. The object is not to impress others but to provide guidance and benchmarks for the future.

A second issue for consideration by consultants is the level of detail in the strategic plan. Consultants probably know what a manager's intent was in writing the plan and thus who is likely to read it, which should provide a clue to the amount of detail needed. Generally, more detail is better. Some owners may resist a lot of detail, but the trend is to provide more information to those within the firm. This is especially true in emerging businesses as most of the employees may be committing many, many hours to the company, and it increases their motivation to understand where the company is headed and what its current status is.

Finally, consultants should encourage clients to communicate the plan to all interested people and to set a specific time for a review of the company's progress. A review should be done at least three to six months after the plan is written but no later than a year after. At least one quarter is necessary for changes in the firm's strategy or environment to be noticeable. Thus, progress should be ascertained at the end of the quarter after the plan is written or at the end of the succeeding quarter. This is not to say that monthly performance should be ignored, but from a strategic viewpoint, a somewhat longer time frame may be more useful. On the other hand, waiting longer than a year to review the company's progress negates the usefulness of the plan. Any time longer than that may reveal so many changes in either the firm's internal status, its strategy, or the economic and competitive environment it faces that no one could determine any cause and effect relationship.

A consultant and the business owner or manager should set a definitive date, approximately a year in advance, to review the plan. Then the consultant—or perhaps the supervising professor in the case of student teams—should keep the date in a tickler file as a reminder to reestablish contact.

It is crucial to write very specific items into the final strategic planning document, a document so detailed and clearly written that all interested parties can understand where the firm is headed and how it plans to get there. In addition, the written document serves as a control measure and an evaluative device at the end of the quarter, fiscal year, or other key time period.

A FINAL COMMENT

We've attempted throughout this book to provide as much information as possible to aid in the creation of a strategic plan for new and emerging businesses. Owners of these businesses are reluctant to take the time necessary to analyze the environment, assess the strengths and weaknesses of the business, and develop a strategic plan based on the distinctive competencies the business possesses. The effort, however, should be highly rewarding, not only because of the strategies actually developed, but because the owner has taken the time to analyze the firm and its environment objectively. This objective analysis alone is worth the time and effort! A written plan provides additional benefits: It encourages commitment to a specific plan, and it offers a mechanism for reviewing progress later. The plan becomes both a measure of success and a method of achieving success. The development and writing of a strategic plan won't guarantee success, but it is a giant stride in that direction.

DISCUSSION QUESTIONS

1. What items should appear in the Business and Its Environment section?
2. How often should the entire strategic plan be rewritten?
3. Are each of the items under the unit goals and strategies section necessary for all firms? Which should always be included and which are optional?
4. What can be done to ensure that the plan is reviewed periodically?
5. How should the plan be shared?

APPENDIX

Sample Strategic Plan
Gaston Ridge Home Health Care, Inc.

The following strategic plan for Gaston Ridge Home Health Care, Inc., provides a sample for readers. Gaston Ridge is a service business operating in the growing and increasingly competitive field of home health care. Although Gaston Ridge's plan is thorough, not every section of the plan is relevant for every business. Service businesses have different styles for plans than do manufacturing businesses. Managers or consultants writing strategic plans should adapt the plan format to their particular needs.

Gaston Ridge Home Health Care, Inc.
Strategic Plan

I. VISION STATEMENT

Gaston Ridge Home Health Care, Inc.'s vision is to be the provider of choice for home health care in the geographic area we serve, while having the respect of clients and their families.

II. MISSION STATEMENT

Gaston Ridge Home Health Care, Inc., provides a full range of quality home health care services to patients in smaller and rural areas of an eight-county licensed service area of southern Illinois.

A. Product Line or Services Provided

Although 15 services are provided, we focus primarily on services prescribed by physicians, such as injections, medications, applications of bandages, etc. To a lesser extent, we educate and train patients and offer occupational and physical therapy. Other services will be added as client demands and expectations arise.

B. Philosophy of the Business

Gaston Ridge operates in a team-oriented manner, with open communication and group consensus guiding major decisions. All employees are encouraged to contribute ideas and suggestions. Gaston Ridge staff spends considerable time and energy building strong relationships with patients and patient families. We are extraordinarily sensitive to the unique needs of patients and their loved ones. Employees are encouraged to build rapport, confidence, and trust as they attend to their patients.

III. THE BUSINESS AND ITS ENVIRONMENT

A. General Environment Characteristics

The senior citizen population is one of the largest groups of individuals in the United States, and this group will grow at an increasing rate as baby boomers move into the retirement years. In particular, the elderly population is rapidly growing, and many in this group will require health care. A significant proportion of them will prefer to receive health care in their home rather than traveling to clinics or residing in nursing homes. Gaston Ridge provides home health care services to patients in small communities and rural sections of an eight-county area of southern Illinois. Most of the current clients are homebound by advanced age or disability.

Expanding technology will continue to affect home health care. Technology will allow us to schedule and control interactions with patients. In addition, technology will increasingly allow procedures such as dialysis, cancer chemotherapy, drug infusion for heart failure, intravenous blood transfusion, and other procedures to be done in patients' homes.

The economy has been expanding in recent years, but its continued expansion is always in doubt. Medicare and Medicaid regulations must be monitored closely for changes that may affect Gaston Ridge. It appears that there will be a continued emphasis in home health care rather than nursing homes and hospitals.

B. Industry Characteristics

Home health care is the fastest-growing segment of health care. Because of the anticipated interaction of political issues, social and demographic changes, and technological advances, the home health care industry should incur significant growth over the next decade. Further, the home health care industry will remain in the growth stage of the product life cycle for some time. Much of this sustained growth is due to the fact that the costs of traditional health care will continue to increase, prompting alternative considerations such as home care.

Gaston Ridge has 16 competitors that operate in at least one of the counties within its service area. However, some of these agencies have only a minor presence. Six major competitor agencies are key players in the area and pose the strongest competitive threat to Gaston Ridge. They are Illini Home Health Care (an affiliate of Illini Medical Center), Capital Center Hospital, Mid-Central Home Health Association, Pioneer Homecare, Cashing Home Health Care, and Senior Dimension Home Care. Both Illini and Capital possess strong services in physical and occupational therapy relative to the competition. However, these services are costly, so their prices are above average. Mid-Central provides meals but quality is perceived as low. No doubt because of their hospital affiliations, Illini and Capital possess strong physician and discharge planner referral bases relative to other competitors. No competitor possesses strong consumer familiarity.

C. Location Description

Gaston Ridge operates in an eight-county service area of southern Illinois. It is located in Perryville, a small community centrally located in the eight-county region. Gaston Ridge is housed in a medical building. The site is used primarily for administrative purposes, although some consultation with families of patients and prospective patients is conducted at this location. The site is acceptable and its central location is critical, because employees need to travel to patients' homes.

IV. DISTINCTIVE COMPETENCIES

The most important distinctive competency is the culture and image of Gaston Ridge. The personal service and attention to building caring relationships with patients and their families differentiates Gaston Ridge from its competitors. Gaston Ridge's considerate approach is valued by consumers and is a key part of Gaston Ridge's approach to its target market. In comparison to Illini Home Health Care and Capital Center, the two most formidable competitors, Gaston Ridge offers more moderate prices.

V. STRATEGY AND GOALS

A. Strategy

Gaston Ridge's strategy is to focus on the needs of homebound patients in rural areas. Services are provided in 15 categories that duplicate many of those provided within a hospital setting. We do not compete in larger cities.

B. Company Goals
1. Horizon Goals
   a. Increase the patient base by 100 percent over the next 3 years.
   b. Increase awareness of Gaston Ridge and the services we offer over the next 3 years so that 90 percent of physicians and 75 percent of the customers in the target market are familiar with us.

2. Near-Term Goals
   a. Develop and implement a new promotional campaign to introduce Gaston Ridge personnel and services to all physicians in the service area within the next 12 months. This goal is segmented into target goals of reaching eight designated physicians every 6 weeks.
   b. Add two physical therapy assistants to the staff within the next year.
   c. Hire a physical therapist as soon as we are sure that the physical therapy client load will reach 35 visits a month.
   d. Provide a meal delivery service in Perryville within the next 6 months.

VI. UNIT-LEVEL STRATEGIES

A. Marketing

1. Target Market

   Gaston Ridge serves an eight-county, 490-square-mile area of southern Illinois. More than 60 percent of Gaston Ridge's market resides in rural areas, with most of the remainder living in small communities. The target market is primarily aged or disabled people who are homebound.

2. Product Line Strategy

   Gaston Ridge Home Health Care, Inc., offers services in 15 areas: new diabetic teaching, venipuncture, intromuscular injections, intravenous therapy, medication teaching, hypertension management, diet instruction, home catheter insertion and maintenance, feeding tubes, postoperative care, wound care, hot/cold applications, physical therapy, occupational therapy, and speech therapy. Physical therapy, occupational therapy, and speech therapy services are contracted through outside sources.

3. Pricing Strategy

   Gaston Ridge's pricing structure is average relative to competitors in the service area.

4. Promotion Strategy

   Minimal advertising is currently done to increase awareness and obtain new patients because of the rural nature of the target market and the lack of a single medium that covers the entire area cost effectively. The following actions comprise the promotion mix:

a. Monthly blood pressure and cholesterol screenings will be conducted in Perryville and the surrounding communities of Ellsworth, Corrington, Wood Ridge, and Brookside. These activities will be arranged through senior citizen centers and local churches. The screenings will be free of charge. Notices of the screenings will be public service advertisements in the local weekly newspapers and radio stations in the area.

b. Informational and goodwill advertising will be placed in the weekly newspapers on a monthly basis.

c. Frequent efforts will be made to inform and influence physicians and their nurses. Gaston Ridge will offer 45-minute breakfast or luncheon meetings with physicians and their nurses at the physician's office. These will be scheduled on Tuesdays and Thursdays, our slow days. These meetings will begin with a 15-minute formal presentation about our services followed by a question-and-answer period. At the conclusion, coffee mugs with the Gaston Ridge logo will be given to the physician and his or her staff. Personalized thank-you notes will be sent the following week. New brochures and follow-up thank-you notes for referrals will be sent every six months.

B. Operations and Human Resources

1. Rene Price, RN, is the administrator and president of Gaston Ridge. She is responsible for payroll, insurance, benefits, and scheduling. Jane Heske, RN, is the director of nursing services. Her responsibilities include Medicare filing, operating the computer, and billing. Michelle Lewis, RN, and Tami Skinner, RN, are case managers in charge of all patients. These four principals each draw a salary from the business.

2. Gaston Ridge employs one full-time health care aide and three part-time health care aides. These women are paid an hourly wage competitive for the industry and area. Physical therapy, occupational therapy, and speech therapy are handled, as needed, on a contractual basis through outside sources. These therapists are also paid an hourly wage.

3. Currently, Gaston Ridge has standard technology and equipment consistent with most of its competitors. However, it does not possess, or does it have ready access to, some of the newer equipment and machines such as mobile EKG and X-ray machines.
4. Clients are billed on an accounts receivable basis. The average accounts receivable collection period is three months after the date of billing.

C. Financial Strategy

Gaston Ridge has received strong community support in the Perryville area and has been able to obtain funds as needed. The county has provided a low-interest loan of $17,000 at 5 percent interest. Further, Legion Bank, located in Perryville, has offered a $20,000 line of credit at 8 percent.

VII. TARGET GOALS AND TARGET ACTION PLAN

1. Design a new physician-focused promotional campaign by July 31.
2. Secure promotional materials and arrangements by August 31.
3. Begin initial promotional contacts by September 15.
4. Determine new job responsibilities for physical therapy assistants and home health aides by August 15.
5. Recruit and hire a full-time additional home health aide and the first physical therapy assistant by September 30.

GLOSSARY

accounts receivable Sales or revenues extended to customers on credit that have not yet been collected.

acid test ratio A liquidity ratio that measures a firm's ability to pay its short-term bills; measured by subtracting inventory from current assets and dividing the result by current liabilities.

activity ratios Ratios that indicate the movement of items through the business and include the inventory turnover ratio and the accounts receivable turnover.

assets Things a company owns that include current assets such as cash, fixed assets such as equipment, and intangible assets such as patents.

average collection period The average amount of days required to collect accounts receivable; calculated as the accounts receivable turnover divided into 365 days.

balance sheet The financial statement that describes the condition of the business; consists of assets, liabilities, and equity.

business plans Either of two major types of plans for a business: The strategic plan focuses on the strategies for the business, and the financial plan focuses on the acquisition and use of funds and is used primarily for acquiring external financing.

cash flow The movement of cash into and out of the business, which, for small and new businesses, is often more important than net income.

company goals Overall goals for a firm that may be either horizon goals or near-term goals.

competitive analysis profile A ranking of a company's competitors based on key industry success factors.

competitive environment   The part of a firm's environment that directly affects the firm and may be affected by the firm's strategy; it includes the firm's customers, competitors, suppliers, and the community in which it operates.

competitive opportunity   A situation in the firm's environment that can be exploited if appropriate firm capabilities exist.

competitive rivalry   The degree to which competitors jockey for position and market share; it is influenced by number and size of competitors and the growth of the industry.

competitive weakness   A weakness in a firm that makes it especially vulnerable to moves of competitors; the opposite of a distinctive competency.

consultant   A person or group that provides advice to a business; may be professionals, not-for-profit, part-time, or student groups.

consulting report   The written or oral presentation to the client outlining the consultant's work and recommendations.

cost containment   Actions taken to reduce or limit costs of operations.

creativity, environment for   A situation in a business in which key players are willing to consider new ideas, take risks, and create innovations.

culture   The tone or climate of a firm; the organizational or corporate culture in a new or emerging firm is strongly affected by the owner and, in turn, affects how the company will address the market in which it competes.

current ratio   The measure of a firm's ability to pay its bills; calculated as current assets divided by current liabilities.

debt-to-assets ratio   A leverage ratio indicating the degree to which assets are funded by debt; measured as total debt divided by total assets.

debt-to-equity ratio   A leverage ratio indicating the percentage of total funding of the business provided by debt; measured by dividing total debt by total equity.

demographic changes   Changes in the makeup of society, particularly regarding the number in particular age brackets, education levels, or income groups.

distinctive competency   A particular strength a company has that significantly surpasses that of competitors.

diversification strategy   A firm's strategy based on an intention to expand into completely different products and markets.

driving forces   Major factors that influence the future direction of an industry, including demand drivers and competitive drivers.

emerging business   A business that is either growing or is poised for growth.

environmental analysis   The analysis of a firm's external environment, including economic, social, technological, political, industry, and competitive factors.

environmental brainstorming   A process for identifying environmental influences.

ETOP (Environmental Threats and Opportunities Profile)   A process for identifying both opportunities and threats by comparing competitors and other environmental situations on a "strong threat" to "strong opportunity" continuum.

equity   The amount of ownership one has in a business; also, the residual when total liabilities are subtracted from total assets.

equity funding   External funding provided in the form of ownership as opposed to debt and may include shares of stock sold to the public or a percentage of ownership held by partners.

external focus   The approach to strategic planning that encourages doing an environmental analysis before doing an internal analysis; the internal analysis is based on identified opportunities and threats.

facilities   Fixed assets usually consisting of plant and equipment, regardless of whether they are owned or leased.

financial ratios   One of the primary means of assessing the financial performance of a firm by comparing two or more items from the firm's balance sheet, cash flow statement, or income statement.

firm analysis   (See **internal analysis.**)

forces for change   Any of a number of external situations that may cause managers to consider the need for new strategies.

general environment   The portion of a firm's environment beyond its capability to affect; includes economic, political, technological, and social factors within the environment. The general environment is differentiated from the industry or competitive environment. Also known as the macroenvironment.

goal　A stated objective for the firm usually expressed in terms of dollars of sales, return on investment, market share, or other financial measure; may be either long-term (horizon) or near-term and may be for the company or one of its units. A goal is to be differentiated from a strategy, which is an action taken to achieve a goal.

gross profit margin　Gross profit (revenues less cost of goods sold) divided by sales.

high (low) margins　A pricing strategy in which the unit price is high (or low) in comparison with the unit cost.

high (low) volume　Typically the result of a low-margin (or high-margin) pricing strategy; volume times margin equals gross profit.

income statement　The financial statement that presents details of a firm's revenues, expenses, and profit or loss; may be calculated on a monthly, quarterly, or annual basis.

incremental change　Changes in products that are minor improvements over existing products.

industry environment　The portion of a company's environment that includes competitors and the industry as a whole.

initial public offering (IPO)　The first offering of a firm's stock to the general public. The process is expensive but may bring in substantial capital for the firm and its owners.

internal analysis　The steps taken to analyze a firm's strengths and weaknesses that should include all aspects of the firm, including its human resources, financial resources, marketing procedures, products, and operations. It is useful to do the analysis in comparison with competitors if possible.

internal analysis profile　A rating of the firm's strengths and weaknesses using a scale such as "strong weakness" to "strong strength."

inventory turnover　An indicator of the speed with which inventory is moving through the firm; measured by dividing cost of goods sold by average inventory.

IPO   (See **initial public offering.**)

just-in-time inventory   An inventory strategy in which components arrive at the company immediately before they are needed rather than being stockpiled.

leverage ratios   Ratios that measure the degree to which a firm is financed through debt rather than equity, including the debt-to-asset ratio and the debt-to-equity ratio.

liabilities   The total debts owed by the firm, including current liabilities and long-term liabilities.

liquidity ratios   Ratios that measure a firm's ability to pay its bills, including the current ratio and quick (acid test) ratio.

loss leaders   Products that are purposely priced below cost in order to attract customers into the store.

management philosophy   The basic philosophy management uses in operating the business and that forms a key part of the firm's mission statement.

market development   A growth strategy in which the firm attempts to expand the market to which it sells its products or services.

market niche   The specific portion of an industry in which a firm competes as well as a portion of the industry market ignored by competitors.

market share   The percentage of total industry sales held by a single firm.

mission statement   A firm's overall and broad guiding statement of purpose that includes the basic description of the firm, its nature, and its philosophy.

operational resources   Those resources that are directly related to producing a firm's products or services.

planning horizon   The length of time into the future that a firm should consider; varies by type of firm and industry.

price elasticity   The sensitivity of a product's volume to changes in price that must be considered in making pricing decisions.

primary information   Information that a manager collects specifically for the analysis being done; may include surveys, product testing, or discussions with managers.

proactive management Management that carefully considers a firm's current and future environment and makes plans to take advantage of developing changes rather than reacting to changes only when they occur.

product development A growth strategy in which a firm develops new variations or improvements of existing products.

product life cycle The variation in the sales of a product as it moves from introduction to growth to stability to decline.

product line The entire offering of a firm's products with broadly similar characteristics. Many small manufacturing businesses offer only a single product line but may have a number of similar products in the line.

product mix The total offering of a firm's products that may consist of a number of product lines.

profitability ratios Ratios that measure a firm's degree of profitability in comparison with sales, assets, or investment, including return on sales, return on assets, and return on investment.

quick ratio (See **acid test ratio.**)

radical change Major changes or new inventions that completely revamp an industry.

reactive management Management that does not plan ahead but instead reacts only to immediate changes in its environment.

relevant business opportunities Opportunities that a business has the capabilities to exploit; not all environmental opportunities are relevant business opportunities.

resistance to change The tendancy of people in a business to maintain the status quo and keep things the way they are.

return on . . . A profitability ratio in which a firm's net income is divided by one of three variables: assets, income, or investment.

secondary information Information that is gathered from already published sources; may include census data, company records, or information from the Internet.

selling strategy The particular strategy used to sell a product to a customer that will vary depending on the type of product and the industry.

statement of work   An agreement between a consultant and a client detailing what tasks will be done by the consultant on behalf of the client; outlines the nature and scope of the project.

stockout   A term describing what happens when a firm is able to sell more of its product(s) than it can produce or buy.

strategic fit   The degree to which a firm's strategy meshes with its basic mission and management philosophy, particularly important when the firm is considering acquiring another firm or introducing a new product.

strategic plan   The document that a company's managers write as a result of the strategic planning process to guide the operation of the firm over the foreseeable future.

strategic planning process   The actions taken to develop a strategic plan and including the premise phase, the analysis phase, and the action phase; the process is perhaps more important than the plan itself.

strategic reaction time   The length of time between an environmental change and a firm's change in strategies to take advantage of it.

sustainable competency   A distinctive competency that can be continued over time and that usually requires either patents, unique designs, or specific skills unable to be duplicated by competitors.

target action plans   Very specific short-run actions to achieve unit or company goals.

target market   The group of customers most likely to buy the firm's products and the group on which the firm should focus most of its marketing resources.

total asset turnover   An activity ratio that measures the extent to which assets are used in the production of goods; measured by dividing sales by total assets.

trade area   The geographical area in which most of a firm's customers reside: may be a few blocks for a grocery store, an entire city for a specialty store, or an entire country or the world for a major manufacturer.

unit goals   The goals of the individual units within the firm that may consist of marketing goals, human resource goals, operations goals, or financial goals; and they may be horizon, near-term, or target goals.

unit strategies   The strategies developed by units within the firm to achieve unit goals and contribute to the overall company strategies and goals.

venture capitalists   Organizations that specialize in providing financing for high-risk, high-return business ventures and that typically insist on significant ownership of the business in exchange for providing equity capital.

vision statement   A statement of some future desirable situation for the business; the overall guiding direction for the firm.

INDEX